Introductic
to the Mac

I0018126

The Photos App

MacOS 13 Ventura Edition

© 2023 iTandCoffee

Special Sales and Supply Queries

For any information about buying this title in bulk quantities, or for supply of this title for educational or fund-raising purposes, contact iTandCoffee on **1300 885 420** or email **enquiry@itandcoffee.com.au**.

iTandCoffee classes and private appointments

For queries about classes and private appointments with iTandCoffee, call **1300 885 420** or email **enquiry@itandcoffee.com.au**.

iTandCoffee operates in and around Camberwell, Victoria in Australia.

Introducing iTandCoffee ...

iTandCoffee is a Melbourne-based business that was founded in 2012, by IT professional Lynette Coulston.

Lynette and the staff at iTandCoffee have a passion for helping others - especially women of all ages - to enter and navigate the new, and often daunting, world of technology and to utilise technology to make life easier, not harder!

At iTandCoffee, **patience is our virtue.**

You'll find a welcoming smile, a relaxed cup of tea or coffee, and a genuine enthusiasm for helping you to gain the confidence to use and enjoy your technology.

With personalised appointments and small, friendly classes – either remotely, in our bright, comfortable, cafe-style space or at your own place - we offer a brand of technology support and education that is so hard to find.

At iTandCoffee, you won't find young 'techies' who speak in a foreign language and move at a pace that leaves you floundering and 'bamboozled'!

Our focus is on helping you to use your technology in a way that enhances your personal and/or professional life – to feel more informed, organised, connected and entertained!

Call on iTandCoffee for help with all sorts of technology – Apple, Windows, Android, iCloud, Evernote, OneDrive, Office 365, Dropbox, all sorts of other Apps, getting you set up on the internet, setting up a printer, and so much more.

iTandCoffee
Relax, we'll help you get iT

Introducing iTandCoffee ...

If you are in small business, iTandCoffee has can help in so many ways – with amazing affordable solutions for your business information needs and marketing.

Here are just some of the topics covered in our regular classes:

- Microsoft Office Products and Microsoft 365 – OneDrive, Word, Excel, PowerPoint
- Introduction to the iPad and iPhone
- A Guided Tour of the Apple Watch
- Bring your Busy Life under Control using your technology.
- Getting to know your Mac and The Photos app on the Mac
- Understanding and using iCloud
- An Organised Life with Evernote
- Taking and Managing photos on the iPhone and iPad
- Managing Photos on a Windows computer
- Windows basics
- Travel with your iPad, iPhone and other technology.
- Keeping kids safe on the iPad, iPhone and iPod Touch.
- Staying Safe Online
- Making the most of your personal technology in your business

The iTandCoffee website (itandcoffee.com.au) offers a wide variety of resources for those brave enough to venture online to learn more: handy hints for iPad, iPhone and Mac; videos and slideshows of iTandCoffee classes; guides on a range of topics; a blog covering all sorts of topical events.

We also produce a regular Handy Hint newsletter full of information that is of interest to our clients and subscribers.

Hopefully, that gives you a bit of a picture of iTandCoffee and what we are about. Please don't hesitate to contact iTandCoffee to discuss our services or to make a booking.

We hope you enjoy this guide and find its contents informative and useful. Please feel free to offer feedback at feedback@itandcoffee.com.au.

Regards,

Lynette Coulston (iTandCoffee Founder)

Introduction to the Mac

The Photos App

TABLE OF CONTENTS

Introduction to the Mac

The Photos App

TABLE OF CONTENTS (cont.)

Introduction to the Mac

The Photos App

TABLE OF CONTENTS (cont.)

Introduction to the Mac
The Photos App
TABLE OF CONTENTS (cont.)

Introduction to the Mac
The Photos App
TABLE OF CONTENTS (cont.)

Introduction to the Mac
The Photos App
TABLE OF CONTENTS (cont.)

Before we start

Introducing the term 'thumbnail' ...

A **thumbnail** is the term used to describe a miniature version of a picture or video.

Thumbnails are used in Photos to help in recognising and organising your photos and videos. Below shows an example of Photo Thumbnails – tapping on a Photo Thumbnail will show you a larger version of the individual photo.

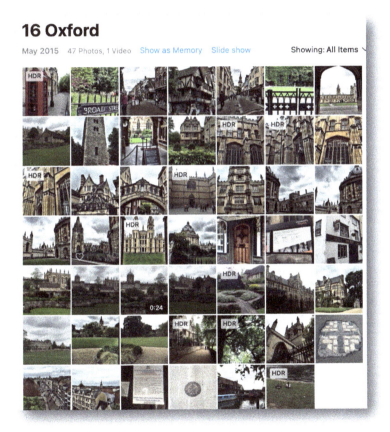

And the term 'metadata'

In a few different places in this document, we will refer to the term 'metadata'. Metadata is the information stored about a photo – where it was taken, when, with what camera/device, file size, resolution, and more.

Before we start

Click, Double-click and Right-Click

Throughout this guide, we will often refer to the 'Click' and 'Right-click' gestures.

Refer to part 1 of this **Introduction to the Mac** series of guides, **A Guided Tour**, for more details of how to set up your Mouse and Trackpad in System Settings to support your Settings for these gestures.

When we refer to 'Click', we are talking about the standard left-click on the Mouse or a single-finger click on the main area of the Trackpad. 'Double-click' means two 'clicks' in quick succession.

(Note. This assumes a 'right-handed' setup for your Mouse! You can set up your Mouse to switch sides for the 'click' and 'right-click' gestures if you are left-handed.)

This 'click' and 'double-click' could instead be a 'tap' or 'double-tap' if you have enabled this feature in the System Settings for your Mouse or Trackpad.

Where there are references to the **'right-click'** gesture, this is referring the 'right-click on the Mouse' gesture – called the **secondary click** in **System Settings -> Mouse,** or **Trackpad**.

This the same gesture as the **Control-click** keyboard shortcut, the **two-finger click** gesture on the trackpad, and the **bottom right corner click** gesture on the trackpad (if you have chosen this instead of the 'two-finger click').

In some places in the document, we mention all of the 'secondary click' gestures when we refer to 'right-click'. But in cases were where we only mention the 'right-click', please substitute the gesture that applies on your own Mac.

Scrolling

For those of you who are using a MacBook and its Trackpad, don't forget that scrolling up and down is achieved by dragging two fingers up and down on your trackpad.

Refer to the guide **A Guided Tour** for more details about setting up your Mac's Trackpad gestures.

Before we start

New in macOS Ventura

Throughout this document, we refer to various changes that have arrived with macOS Ventura. Below are specific sections that discuss some of the more significant changes (as well as the corresponding page number).

Introducing Photos

The **Photos** app on your Mac provides a place to manage all your Photos and videos – your 'library' of photos (and videos.)

By importing all photos and videos using the **Photos** app (into your **Photos Library**), it is then possible to view, organise and share them in multiple ways.

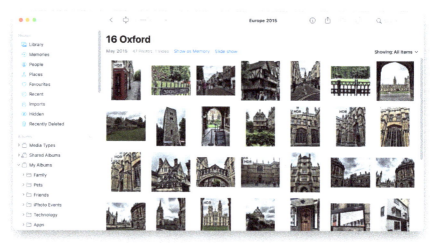

Photos (and videos) can be viewed on a **timeline,** allowing a 'drill-down' to a photo or set of photos based on when the photo was taken – starting first with **Years**, then **Months** within a Year, and then **Days** within the month. We'll look at this 'timeline' view shortly.

Photos and videos can also be viewed as 'Memories', by places, people and other 'albums', presented in slide shows, shared with others via iCloud, and more.

Your other Mac applications can use your photos/videos and albums that are stored in your **Photos** library - for example, when inserting a photo in your email, the search screen allows you to browse **Photos** for the image you wish to include.

It is important to understand that, while a particular photo may appear under more than one 'album' or in more than one of the library areas in Photos, that photo **exists only once in the library**.

When you place a photo into an album, **you are not moving it or copying it**. We'll talk about this in more detail throughout this guide.

A Guided Tour of Photos

Let's look first at the various areas of the Photos App. For those of you who used Photos under MacOS Sierra or earlier, you will notice that there are quite a few changes in the subsequent versions of Photos.

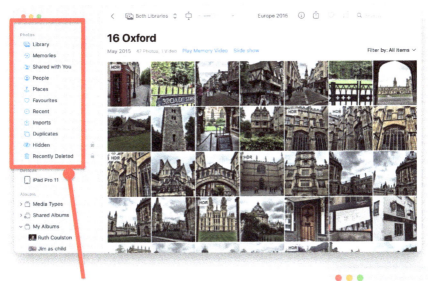

The Sidebar

Let's look first at the Sidebar on the left.

In Sierra and earlier, the sidebar was something that could be turned on and off (from the View menu). Since High Sierra, it has been a permanent fixture.

The main sections in the Photos sidebar are Photos, Albums, and Projects.

Let's look at the different sections shown in the Sidebar.

Before we do, it is important to note that the content of each section in the sidebar can be hidden.

If you are only seeing the name of any section and not its contents, hover the mouse over the section name and click the symbol >.

In the same way, you can hide the contents of each section by hovering over the section name and clicking the symbol ∨.

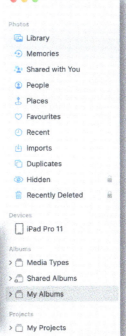

A Guided Tour of Photos

Photos

The top section of the sidebar is Photos, which provides several options for viewing your photos, each of which we will cover in more detail in subsequent pages.

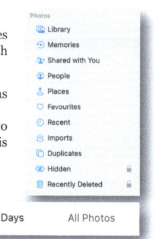

Library   View your whole photos library as timeline, based on 'Date Taken'.
Options along the top allow you to choose different ways to view this full collection of photos:

Years	Months	**Days**	All Photos

Years	View your photos grouped by Year
Months	View your photos grouped by Month
Day	View your photos grouped by Day
All Photos	View your timeline of photos ungrouped

Memories   The Photos app will automatically create 'curated collections' of your photos, to help you re-discover forgotten memories buried in your photos. Visit this option regularly to see your new 'Memories'.

Shared with You (New in macOS Ventura)
This new option shows the photos that others have shared with you via Messages. Choose to save them to your Library by right-clicking and choosing **Save 1 shared photo**.

People   The Photos app helps you identify and group photos of people, so that you can view collections of photos for the various people in your life. (This option used to appear under the Albums section in the Sierra version of Photos.)

Places   View your photos on a map, based on the location that was recorded against the photo when it was taken. (This option used to appear under the Albums section in the Sierra version of Photos.)

Zoom in and out on this map to 'split out' your photos by their location. It is a great way of seeing all the places you have been!

Favourites   View those photos you have marked as your 'Favourites'. (This option used to appear under the Albums section in the Sierra version of Photos.)

12

A Guided Tour of Photos

Recents   Your photos listed in the order in which they appeared on this Mac (instead of their 'date taken' order). So, if you just saved a photo to your Mac from, say, an email, it will appear as the last photo – even it that photo was taken a while ago.

Imports   Imports allows you to view your photos according to when they were imported.

Hidden   This album will only appear if you have chosen to Hide any of your photos from the other views. This is handy for photos that you don't really want other to see. I use it to hide screenshots that I was taking of regular Speed Tests of my internet, which I don't want clogging up my Timeline and other views.

Recently Deleted

Deleted photos are moved to this area and retained for around 30 days, after which they are deleted.

Devices

This section will show if you have plugged in an external device (e.g. an iPhone or iPad) or when you are in the process of importing a set of photos. Click on the Device to see the set of photos and choose what to import (more on this soon).

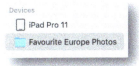

Albums

The Albums section has undergone many changes over time.

Some of the albums that previously 'lived' in this section were moved up under the 'Library' section (Favourites, People, Places, Imports, Recently Deleted) in the transition from Sierra to later versions.

The Albums area is separated into three main sub-sections – **Media Types, Shared Albums** and **My Albums**.

A Guided Tour of Photos

Media Types groups your photos according to their type – videos, selfies, live photos, etc. Photos will automatically appear in these albums based on their format/type. You cannot choose what goes in these albums – and some albums will be missing if there are no photos of that type in the library.

Shared Albums includes the photos and Albums found in your iCloud **Shared Albums** area – reflecting albums you have shared with other or that others have shared with you. You can also see the Activity that has occurred with these Shared Albums – additions, comments, etc. This section will only appear if you have chosen to enable **Shared Albums** in your iCloud settings. This is covered more fully a bit later.

The **My Albums** sub-section contains the Folders and Albums that you create, something that we cover in more detail later.

Projects

The final section of the sidebar is the **Projects** section, listing any projects you have created using your photos – photo books, calendars, card, slideshows, prints.

Toolbar options

In most views of the Photos app, you will notice a set of symbols at the top right. Let's look at the meaning of these symbols – we'll then cover these things in more detail later.

Show information about the photo that is currently selected. This information includes the camera it was taken with, when it was taken, its size, location, and perhaps the people in it. For some photos (e.g of dogs, plants, flowers, etc), this information may include additional information about the subject.

A Guided Tour of Photos

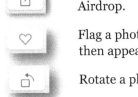

Share a photo (or set of photos) – for example, via Message, Mail or Airdrop.

Flag a photo (or several photos) as being a 'favourite' – these photos then appear in the Favourites area of the 'Library' section

Rotate a photo by 90°. Keep clicking until orientation is as desired.

Search for photos by date, categories, keywords, people, and more. As an example, type 'dog' in this search field to find all photos with a dog.

Filter By

In many views of thumbnails of your photos – Albums, All Photos, Recents and various other place, you will see the **Filter By** option on the top right-hand side, below the Search bar.

This option allows you to choose to filter the photos you are viewing, to only see Favourites, or only Edited photos, only Photos, or only Videos.

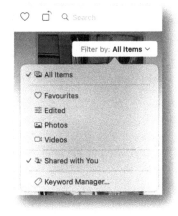

Viewing your Photo Library On A TimeLine

All of our photos have a 'date taken' associated with them, recorded by the camera or smartphone/tablet when the photo was taken. (For a camera, this means that the date must have been correctly set at that point in time.)

Information like 'date-taken' is known as the **metadata** associated with your photos. Location information can also be recorded as part of your photo's metadata, depending on the device used to take the photo; camera type will also be recorded.

The Photos app uses the 'date taken' and 'location' information to show your photos on a timeline, allowing you to view all the photos taken by **Year**, then **Month**, then by individual **Days** or sets of days and places. You can also view **All Photos** in date order.

(Note. In macOS Catalina in 2019, this 'Years, Months, Days, All Photos' naming/grouping of the photos in this area replaced the previous 'Photos, Moments, Collections, Years' naming/grouping that had applied previously.)

Years   Months   Days   All Photos

Clicking the **Library** option in the sidebar provides the ability to view this timeline of photos listed according to these groupings.

The four options are shown along the top when the Library option is selected in the Sidebar. Let's look now at these four ways of viewing your photos timeline.

Viewing your Photo Library On A TimeLine

Years   Years   Months   Days   All Photos

The **Years** view shows large 'thumbnails' of each the years that are represented by your collection of photos, according to each photo's 'date taken'.

(Note. We'll cover later how you can adjust this 'date taken' so that photos with incorrect dates – eg. scanned old photos – appear in the correct place on this timeline.)

Double-click on any of these thumbnails to view the photos represented by that year, grouped by month.

Months   Years   Months   Days   All Photos

Months view provides a summary of photos, listed in Month order – with large thumbnails to represent collections of photos within each month.

Double-click on any of these large thumbnails to view the associated photos.

Click the symbol ⊙ at top right of the thumbnail. You will see the options:

- **Play Memory Movie** to view a slideshow (with music) of the set of photos or
- **Show Map** to view the set of photos on a map (if any location metadata is available for the photos)

To see all the photos associated with the month and surrounding months, click the **All Photos** option when you have the applicable month in view.

Viewing your Photo Library On A TimeLine

Days

Years   Months   **Days**   All Photos

The **Days** view provides individual photos, or thumbnails representing the photos taken on a particular date or set of dates.

Double-click on any **thumbnail** of a photo in your **Days** view to view that individual photo.

To see all the photos associated with that day and surrounding days, click the **All Photos** option when you have the applicable date in view.

If you see a number in an oval at the bottom right of a thumbnail (as shown right), this means there are a number of further photos associated that date. Click the number to view those photos.

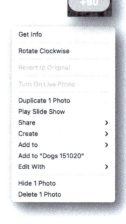

Right-click (or two-finger click) any photo's thumbnail to see a menu of options that apply to the selected photo (see right).

In the **Days** view, you will also see a 'zoom' slider in the top bar, towards the left (near the 'traffic lights').

This slider allows the size of the thumbnails to be enlarged and reduced to suit your requirements – handy when you are searching for a photo or comparing similar photos.

Viewing your Photo Library On A TimeLine

All Photos

Years Months Days **All Photos**

The **All Photos** view allows for the viewing of all photos by 'date taken'.

If you have a Month or Day in view when you click the All Photos option, the set of photos you see first in All Photos relate to that Month/Day.

Use the slider at the top left to adjust the size of the thumbnails you see.

As shown below, the thumbnails can be made very small, to allow you to scan for a point in time and photo.

Double-click on any thumbnail to view the photo, then use your arrow keys to move through the photos before and after that photo.

19

Other options for viewing your Library

People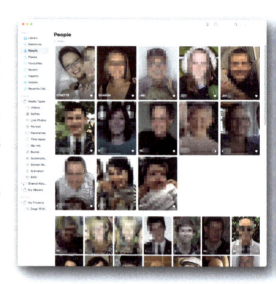

This special album splits photos into groupings according to facial recognition.

Those people you deem your 'favourites' can be shown at the top, and you can 'merge' sets of photos that the Photos app has matched, to build up comprehensive set of photos of each person.

We'll cover this more fully a bit later in this guide.

Places

The Places view of your photos Library shows your photos according to the location at which they were taken – for those photos that have location information stored in their metadata. Along the top of this view, you will see three options – **Map**, **Satellite** and **Grid** – providing different ways of viewing the groupings of your photos by 'place'.

In **Map** view, thumbnails of photos are shown on a map, where each thumbnail shows the number of photos taken at each location. Double-click on any of these thumbnails to view those photos.

Zoom in and out on this map to 'split out' your photos by their location.

Use the – and + at the bottom right of the screen to zoom.

Satellite view is very similar to **Map** view – except that it shows your photos on a satellite image, on which you can then zoom in to see birds-eye views of where your photos were taken.

Other options for viewing your Library

This is an amazing feature, allowing you to revisit the places where your photos were taken.

Grid view shows the photos of places as thumbnails, grouped by location.

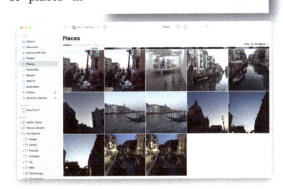

View an individual photo by double-clicking on it.

Or Click on the > next to the location to view the location's photos in **Explore View**

Favourites   Favourites

Favourites shows any photos you've marked as being favourites –

- by clicking the heart icon at the top when viewing the individual photo, or
- by clicking the heart in the bottom left corner of the thumnail as you hover over the applicable thumbnail.

To remove a favourite, just click on it (or on several) and click the heart symbol in the toolbar at top right. The 'un-favoured' photos will disappear from the Favourites view.

If you use iCloud to sync your Photos, the same set of Favourites will appear across all your devices – i.e. they will sync.

Other options for viewing your Library

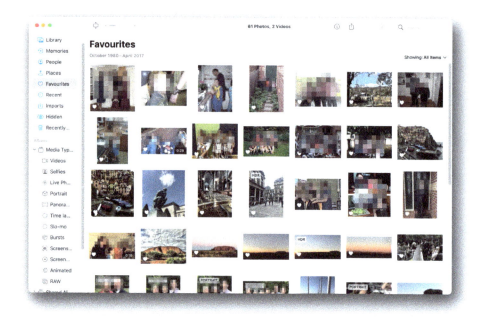

If you are not using iCloud Photos (covered towards the end of this guide), **Favourites** you have chosen on your iPad or iPhone are separate to those on your Mac. This means that, even if you have 'hearted' a photo on you iPhone, it won't automatically appear in Favourites on your Mac (or your iPad, for that matter).

(iCloud Photos users will find that syncing of Favourites DOES occur between devices.)

Recent   Recent

The **Recent** option arrived in macOS Catalina in 2019 and provides the ability to view your photos according to date they 'arrived on' the Mac.

This means that the order you see here may be different to that you see in the **Library** views described earlier, since a photo taken several years ago but just saved to Photos will appear as the last photo in Recent.

To see any photo from the **Recent** view in its 'date' order (and with other photos taken on the same or adjacent dates), right click on the photo in **Recent** and choose **Show in All Photos**

Other options for viewing your Library

Imports   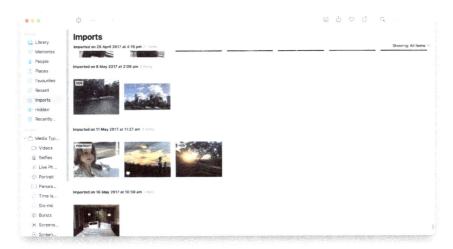 Imports

The Imports view in Library shows the photos according to the date they were imported to your Mac from a Camera, SD Card, iPhone or iPad, or any another import method – see later in this guide for methods of importing photos you your Photos library.

Hidden   Hidden

The **Hidden** album includes any photos you have chosen to **Hide** from the casual observer!

Photos that you Hide are not shown in other Library views.

To Hide, right-click (or two-finger-click) on any photo (or a set of photos) and choose **Hide 1 Photo** or **Hide *n* Photos** (where '*n*' is the number of photos you have selected).

Photos lets you then choose whether the **Hidden** album appears under the Library section. It can remain out of sight if you desire.

Go to the **View** menu in the top menu bar and choose **Hide Hidden Photo Album** to hide it or **Show Hidden Photo Album** to include it under Library

Other options for viewing your Library

Recently Deleted   🗑 Recently Deleted

Just as it sounds, the Recently Deleted album holds photos you have decided to 'trash'.

The Photos App retains deleted photos and videos for about 30 days (sometimes up to 40 days), in case you make a mistake and need to retrieve them.

Photos in this album show the days remaining before permanent deletion.

Recently Deleted   Recover   Delete All

To permanently delete the photos from this album (and thereby free up their allocated storage), just choose **Delete All** (which will be at top right) when viewing this Album.

Recently Deleted   Recover   Delete 4 Photos

Alternatively, if you find you have deleted a photo or video in error, just select **Recently Deleted**, select the applicable photo/s (by clicking on it/them), and choose **Recover** (at top right).

New for Hidden and Deleted Albums in macOS Ventura

The Hidden and Deleted albums are now protected by your Mac's password, so that you can be sure that there is no unauthorised access to the photos in this area. The same applies on your iPad and iPhone.

When you click on either of these albums, you will now see an authentication screen appear – asking you to provide Touch ID authentication (if application) or enter the Mac's password.

Only after authentication will the content of the album appear.

If you don't require such protection for these albums, go to **Photos -> Settings** and untick the **Privacy** option in the General area.

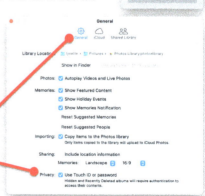

24

Viewing individual photos/videos

Getting to a single photo/video

From any view that shows 'thumbnails' of your photos, **double-click** on any image's thumbnail to view the individual photo.

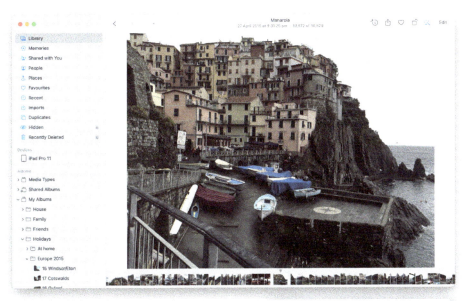

Alternatively, if an item is already selected (i.e. it has a blue border around it), press the space bar to view that item. Pressing the space bar again will then bring you back to the thumbnail view.

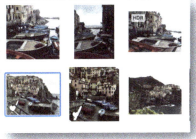

(This is the equivalent of Quick Look in Finder for quickly viewing file contents.)

Then, use the right and left arrow keys on your keyboard to move to the next or previous photo.

Alternatively, you can swipe left or right using your Apple Mouse or Trackpad (use two fingers on the Trackpad.

Zoom in and out when viewing the photo using the slider at top left of the screen.

Viewing individual photos/videos

Returning to previous 'view'

Use the < symbol at top left to go 'back up' to the previous level (eg. back to the applicable Thumbnail view).

Double-clicking on the individual photo that you are viewing will have the same effect as clicking the < symbol.

View in Full Screen

To view your photo or video in full-screen mode, click the green traffic light.

Press Esc to on your keyboard to exit full-screen mode. (See part 3 of this guide series for more on using full screen and part-screen mode.)

If you don't want to see the thumbnails along the bottom while viewing in full screen, choose **Hide Thumbnails** from the **View** menu.

Play a video

If the item is a video, you will see a bar of symbols when you bring the mouse pointer over the image on the screen.

- *To play a video:* Click the 'Play' symbol ▶

- *To stop a video:* Click the double bars ‖

Explore view

The **Explore** view allows you to look at where a photo was taken on a map, to view other 'nearby photos', and to see other 'related' photos.

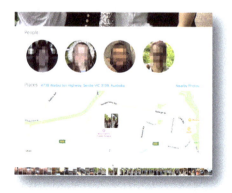

The look of this 'view' is very similar to the 'Memories' view, described in the next section.

To see the *Explore* view, **scroll up** while viewing an individual photo.

Viewing individual photos/videos

Make sure you 'Heart' your favourites

You may have noticed that the bar of options that is visible when viewing individual photos includes the ♡ option.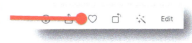

The ♡ option allows you to specify certain photos as your 'Favourites'.

Click on this heart to 'Favourite' a photo that you are currently viewing. The photo will then automatically appear in the **Favourites** album.

Any photo that has been set as a 'Favourite' will show a shaded heart. 💙 Just click the heart again to remove the photo from your Favourites.

See any photo with other photos from that same day

This is something I find very handy, especially when checking for duplicated photos or wanting to check what other similar photos exist for a photo I have put in an album or that appears in my **All Photos** view.

If you are viewing a photo in a view other than Days/All Photos (either as a full thumbnail or in individual photo view), right-click (or two-finger-click) on it and choose **Show in All Photos**

This will take you straight to the **All Photos** view, with the selected photo highlighted with a blue border, and showing all the other photos taken on and around the same date.

Memories -
Re-visit your past through photos

The Memories option was introduced to the Photos app by Mac OS Sierra and iOS 10, late in 2016.

Here is how Apple describes this feature:

> *"Rediscover favourite and forgotten moments from deep in your photo library. Memories automatically creates curated collections of your most meaningful photos and videos."*

The contents of the **Memories** area will be chosen for you automatically by the Photos app, from (supposedly) the best photos in the library (although I'm not convinced this is always true!).

You will see 'Memories' like those shown in the screen shots on the right. Just double-click on a particular Memory you wish to view

Memories have changed in macOS Ventura

Prior to Ventura, double-clicking on a Memory gave you a screen like that on the right – and you could choose the 'Play' symbol to start the slideshow.

The photos that are included in the Memory showed beneath the larger slideshow thumbnail.

In macOS Ventura, the slideshow with music starts straight away, and the screen looks like the example on the right – showing controls and thumbnails of the included photos along the bottom.

To see a grid of the photos that are in the Memory, click the symbol at bottom right.

On left of that symbol is the Play/Pause icon

Memories -
Re-visit your past through photos

Restarts the slideshow.

Choose the music for the Memory slideshow (from entire Apple Music library)

Choose a 'Look' for the slideshow (i.e. apply a filter)

The Controls and thumbnails will disappear after a short while. Click on the screen to make them re-appear.

The type of memories that appear can be controlled from **Photos -> Settings**.

In the **General** area, there is a section with Memories options. Untick any of the options that you don't want. Suggested Memories and People can also be reset using the options provided.

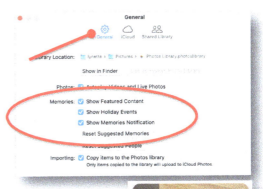

Right-click on any memory to see a variety of options for the Memory – including **Favourite** or **Unfavourite** and **Delete Memory**.

You can also provide feedback on the type of Memories you don't like by choosing **Feature Fewer Memories Like This**.

While the slideshow is visible, there are also a few further options available at top right, including some that are available by clicking the ⊙ .

Choose a particular photo to **Make Key Photo** – i.e. the photo that appears as the Memory thumbnail - and choose the duration for each photo (Short or Medium) in the slideshow.

Choose the heart symbol to make the Memory a Favourite.

To view just your **Favourite Memories**, choose that option along the top of the Memories view.

Selecting Photos

Before we get into talking about creating your own albums, we need to cover a couple of other things relating to managing your photos – selecting photos and deleting photos.

Quite often, you will have the need to select more than one photo – for example, to select a set of photos to add to an album, to delete, to put in a slideshow, to share and more. There are several ways to select photos:

Select a single photo   Just click on a thumbnail or double-click to open that photo.

Select multiple random photos: Multiple random photos can be selected (and unselected) in photo thumbnail view by **holding down the Command Key** as you click on each item in the view.

Select inclusive range of photos: An inclusive range of photos can be selected by clicking the first photo in the range and then, as you click the last photo in the range, **holding down the Shift key**.

Select all photos: Click any image in the thumbnail view and then choose **Command-A** (select all) to select all in that view.

Unselect selected photos: If you have selected multiple photos, you can then **unselect** certain of these photos by **holding down the Command Key** as you click the photo/s.

Selected photos are indicated with a blue border.

Refer to this page whenever we talk about selecting multiple photos throughout this guide.

Deleting photos

Understanding 'Delete' vs 'Remove'

Photos can be **Deleted** a few different ways.

But before we discuss these methods, we need to first look at the difference between 'Removing' a photo from an Album and 'Deleting' a photo.

Always make sure you check the message that appears when you are deleting, to confirm if you are actually 'deleting' or 'removing'. What do I mean by this?

If you are looking in one of the Photos areas, or in a Media Types album, or in a 'Smart Album', and you choose to Delete any of the photos in view, you will be **deleting** the photos from the Photos Library.

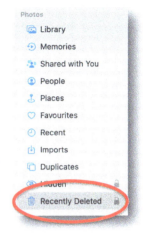

They will go into the **Recently Deleted** album and be permanently deleted after 30 days (approx.).

If you are looking at a set of photos that are in a **My Albums** *album, one that you have created* (we'll look at creating your own albums shortly), and you hit the Delete key or choose 'Remove' from the right-click menu', you will just be 'removing' the photo/s from that Album but leaving them in the Photos library and in any other Album that you have added them to.

If you are going through a process of deleting unwanted photos from your Photos library, it is best to be viewing one of the **Library** or **Media Types** views, not viewing them in an Album you created yourself.

Ways to Delete

1. If you are viewing an individual photo in one of the Library views or in Media Types, select the **delete** key on the keyboard, then confirm by selecting the **Delete** button from the message that appears.

2. Right-click (or two-finger-click) on the selected photo/s (refer earlier for methods of selecting multiple photos) and choose the **Delete** option from the list of options that appear. You will see the same confirmation message that appeared in option 1 – select **Delete** to confirm

3. If you want to delete without having to confirm, select one or more photos (refer earlier) and choose ⌘-**delete (Command-Delete)** on the keyboard.

Deleting Photos

Removing photos from your own Albums

When you are viewing photos in an album that you have created, just select the Delete key on the keyboard to **Remove** the photo from the album.

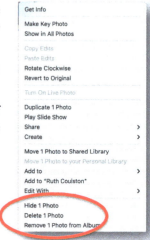

The photo will **not** be removed from any other Albums and it will **not** be deleted from the Library.

If you truly want to delete a photo that appears in one of your own albums – and delete it completely from the library as well - you can

- choose ⌘–**delete (Command-Delete)** or

- Right-click and choose the **Delete** option at the bottom.

Where do Deleted photos go?

As mentioned earlier, deleted photos and videos will be moved to the **Recently Deleted** album.

If a photo was incorrectly deleted, go to the **Recently Deleted** album, select the photo or photos, and choose **Recover** (top right).

Photos 'removed' from a personal album or Memory will still be available in the Photos library and can be re-added to the album/Memory if required.

Some hidden space gobblers to delete

If you have a newer iPhone or iPad – one that is capable of taking 'Bursts', you may find yourself with quite a few 'bursts' of several photos, instead of just the single photo that you want.

Visit the **Bursts** album under **Media Types** to find and eradicate these extra photos.

In the example shown on right, there are several sets of 'bursts' in the **Bursts** album.

To save space, you can choose the best from each set of photos and delete the rest.

To do this, double-click to view one of the 'bursts'. At top left of

Deleting Photos

the photo is **Make a Selection**. Click this to view the full set of photos in the burst.

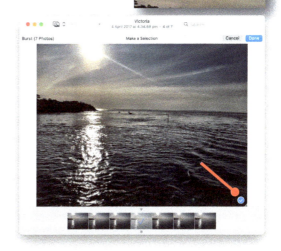

Along the bottom shows a ribbon of the photos in the burst.

Use the arrow keys (or click on thumbnails) to move through the thumbnails and compare them – and tick (at bottom right of photo) the photo/s that you wish to keep.

Choose **Done** when you have finished the selection.

The above message will appear – giving you the option to just keep the selected photos, or to keep everything in the burst.

Usually, you will choose **Keep Only Selection**, so that the rest of the photos can be moved to **Recently Deleted**.

A Handy Tip if you make a mistake when deleting

Don't forget that, in most cases, you can **Undo your last action** – for example, restore incorrectly deleted photos – by simultaneously pressing the two keys.

⌘-Z (Command-z)

The **Edit** menu provides the same 'Undo' option, in case you forget this keyboard combination. It even shows you exactly what the ⌘-Z combination will 'Undo'.

Also available in the Edit menu is the **Redo** option, should you decide that you need to reverse the 'Undo'.

The exception to this is if you Delete your photos from the **Recently Deleted** album. This <u>**cannot**</u> be undone.

Introducing Albums

As mentioned earlier, the Photos app allows for the organising of photos (and videos) by arranging them into **Albums**, or for viewing of photos in standard Albums that Apple has provided for you.

Albums that you create can then be grouped into 'Folders' – providing a great way of being able to find the photos you are looking for.

If you don't see anything listed in the Albums area of your sidebar, hover the mouse pointer over the word **Albums** and click the > symbol that appears on the right.

As described earlier, the **Albums** section includes three major sub-sections – **Media Types**, **Shared** and **My Albums**

> ☐ Media Types

> ☐ Shared Albums

> ☐ My Albums

Media Types contains albums that group photos according to their type. This occurs automatically, based on each photo's metadata.

The Media Types albums cannot be deleted and will only appear if you have any photos of the type represented by that album.

Lets look first at these **Media Type** albums that are provided by Apple.

We'll look at the **Shared** section when we talk about iCloud, and the **My Albums** section when we talk later about how to organise your photos.

Albums - Media Types

To view the full set of **Media Types** albums, click on the ⟩ that is on its left – this will expand the list of albums under this area.

As already mentioned, the set of albums you see listed under **Media Types** will depend on the photos that are in your Library. This means that you may not see the full set of albums shown on the right.

Here are the possible albums that will appear:

Videos

As you can probably guess, the Videos album shows all the videos that are in your Photos Library.

Selfies

This album shows any photos in the library that were taken with the front camera of your iPad or iPhone (or the Facetime camera on your Mac).

Screenshots

This album shows any 'screen shots' found in your library – whether they were taken on your iPad, iPhone (assuming iCloud Photos is turned on) or on the Mac.

We often end up with lots of superfluous screen shots, so it is worth a visit to this Media Type album to delete those you don't need.

Live Photos, Panoramas, Slo-Mo, Time Lapse and Bursts, Portrait, Animated, RAW, Screen Recordings, Long Exposure

These albums show any photos that you took with your iPad/iPhone and using the corresponding feature from that device.

Organising your Photos -
Find your People

The **People** album under **Library** offers a great way of viewing all the photos of a particular person, using facial recognition to discover and group photos.

The first time you visit the People album, your Photos app will show a set of thumbnails that represent groups of photos that have been determined as showing the same person. Double-click on any of these thumbnails to view the set of photos that have been found for that person.

Name your people

By hovering the mouse pointer over a photo's thumbnail, you will see appear at the bottom left of the thumbnail.

Click here to assign a name to the person.

A list of suggested contacts will appear below – just click on the relevant person, or (if they are not a Contact) keep typing the name and choose enter/return to complete.

At that point, you may see another screen appear, asking for confirmation of some other faces that are deemed to be close matches to the person in the thumbnail that you just named.

Organising your Photos - Find your People

Select (by clicking circle at bottom right of each thumbnail to tick/un-tick) those thumbnails that are the same person as that you named, and then choose **Done**.

This will collate even more photos of that same person.

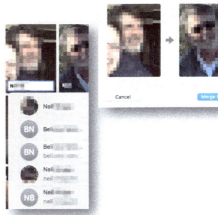

If you name the person in the thumbnail and it is found that there is already a named thumbnail for that same person, the screen below right will appear, asking for confirmation that the two thumbnails represent the same person.

If they do, select **Merge Photos**, which will merge the two sets of photos into one. Otherwise, select **Cancel**

Remove unwanted people

You will probably see the faces of people you barely know or are not really important to you.

These faces can be removed from the People album.

Right-click (or two-finger-click) on the thumbnail and choose the option **Remove this Person.**

Confirm by selecting **Remove from People Album** when you see the confirmation message below.

Organising your Photos - Find your People

Nominate your favourites

Your most important people can be 'hearted' by clicking the small heart at the bottom right of each thumbnail, or by right-clicking on a thumbnail in People and choosing **Favourite this Person**.

This nominates that the person is a 'favourite'.

Favourites then appear at the top of the People screen, as larger thumbnails than the rest.

Identifying more photos of the same person

For each identified 'Person', double-click the thumbnail on the main People screen to view the 'already-matched' photos of that person, shown as a 'Memories' style screen with lots of ways of viewing photos of the person.

You may see a message at the top of this view – advising that there are additional photos that could be

of the same person.

Here is what just came up for my own People album. Untick any thumbnails that are not the person, then choose Done.

Scroll down that screen to see some additional options at the very bottom.

Click Confirm Additional Photos to look for more photos of the same person.

You will then be taken through a series of photos and asked to confirm if each one is (or is not) the applicable person. Click **Yes** if the photos <u>IS</u> of the person, and **No** otherwise.

Organising your Photos - Find your People

Choose **Done** in the top bar to finish, or wait until you have exhausted all the possible potential matches.

You will see the total number of additional photos that you just added for that person.

Confirming just a few additional matches can add a substantial number of photos to the set collated for that person.

You've added 574 photos of J̶̶̶n.

Merge People

If you see more than one thumbnail for the same person, the sets of photos represented by these thumbnails can be merged.

Select the applicable thumbnails (using the *command* key as you click each), then right-click (or two-finger-click) on one of them to see this list of options.

Choose **Merge n People** (where n is the number of thumbnails you selected) to combine. You will see the below confirmation message. Select **Yes** to complete the merging process.

Identifying people while viewing photos

There is another way of updating your People album and adding to the photos for each of your people.

While you are viewing individual photos, you can turn on a feature that shows the name of each identified person in the photo and shows **unnamed** for anyone who hasn't been identified yet.

Go to the **View** menu at the top and choose **Show Face Names.**

Click on **unnamed** under any faces that are not yet identified, and type in the name of the person.

Organising your Photos - Find your People

If someone is incorrectly identified, type in their correct identity in the box under their face.

Turn off this feature again by visiting the **View** Menu and choosing **Hide Face Names.**

When the wrong person appears in a People album

Of course, the face recognition technology is not perfect – so you may find that, when you have a look at the set of photos for a person, there are photos of other people included.

It is easy to remove any incorrectly matched photos from a People album.

Double-click on the person's thumbnail to view the set of photos of that person.

For any photo or photos that does not belong, right click (or two-finger-click) on the photo/s and choose ***Person-name*** **is not in this photo**

Make Key Photos

To change the photo that is used as the 'thumbnail' for a person in the screen showing your collection of People, find the photo that you prefer, right-click on it (or two-finger click, if applicable) and choose **Make Key Photo**.

Sort People by Name (new in macOS Ventura)

When you build up a large set of People, it can be hard to find someone you are looking for.

The good news is that you can now sort the People album in alphabetical order – making this much easier.

Go the **View** menu while in the People thumbnails view and hover the mouse pointer over **Sort**, then click **Keep Sorted by Title** so that it shows a tick on the left side. You can also choose Ascending vs Descending order.

Organising your Photos - Creating an Album

Many of us end up with a huge number of photos on our Mac.

While the timeline functionality in the Photos view, and the Memories, People, Places and other features allow us to find the photos we are looking for, most of us want to also organise our photos into our own Albums, albums that contain the photos for a particular occasion, holiday, person, place or other grouping.

Albums offer a great way of showcasing your photos to family and friends, and a great way of organising your images so that you can find them when you need them! A photo can appear in multiple Albums that you create.

Create an album

Before you create an album, it is important to decide if you want to create an 'empty' album (and add photos after its creation), or whether you want to select some photos and then create an album for those photos.

If you want an empty album, just ensure that you don't have any photos selected. If any photos have a blue border around them (indicating they are in the current selection), just click in the white space surrounding the photos to cancel the current selection.

There are then several ways to create a new album.

Option 1: From the menu bar, select
File -> New Album

Option 2: Hover the mouse pointer over **My Albums** in the sidebar, and you will see a + on the right. Click this +, then click Album to create a new album.

Option 3: Right-click on **My Albums** (or on any Folder that you have already created in My Albums) and choose **New Album**

Organising your Photos - Creating an Album

Option 4: If you have some photos selected, right-click (or two-finger-click) and choose **Add to** (or find the same option in the **Image** menu). You will then see a list of options – click the first option, **New Album**.

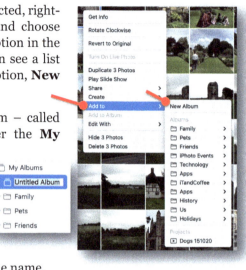

For each of these options, a new album – called **Untitled Album** - will appear under the **My Albums** section in the sidebar.

If it is already highlighted in blue (as on right), simply type in the name for the new album.

If the name is not highlighted, click once to select the album, then again to get into 'edit' mode to change the name.

Or right-click on the un-named album and choose **Rename Album.**

We will also shortly cover how to create **Folders**, which are collections of albums (and, perhaps, folders).

If you already have folders in your My Albums area, it is easy to add an album to that folder.

Just click on the folder and choose the + symbol that appears on the right side.

Organising your Photos - Adding Photos/Videos to an Album

Adding photos to an existing album is very easy – there are several ways to achieve this.

Use Drag and Drop

One way to add photos to an existing album is to simply select one or more photos and drag them on top of the name of the Album in the sidebar.

A blue background will appear across the Album Name to show that it is the one that is selected. If you let go, the selected photos will 'drop into' that album.

Use Add to

You can also add to an existing album by right-clicking (or two-finger-clicking) on any of the selected photos and choosing **Add to**.

(This **Add to** option is also available from the **Image** menu.)

From the list shown, choose the album to which the photos should be added.

In the example on the below, I had to hover over the Folder called 'Us' to allow me to select one of the albums within that folder.

We'll talk about Folders shortly.

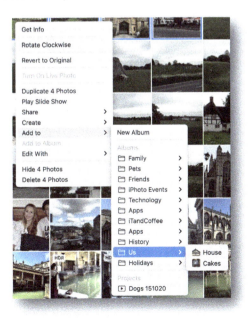

Organising your Photos - Managing Albums

Renaming an Album

If you want to rename an existing Album, just right-click on it in the Sidebar and choose '**Rename Album**', then enter the new name for the Album.

Or, if viewing the albums as 'Thumbnails', just click on the name underneath the thumbnail, and change.

Rearranging Albums

Albums can be listed in the order that you choose. Just click and drag the Album to the required location.

A blue line (see right) will show the position where the Album will be moved – just release the mouse or trackpad to 'drop' the Album to that position.

If you are viewing the albums as thumbnails, just click and drag the Album thumbnail to the required position.

The other albums will 'move aside', and you can 'drop' the album in the space that is made.

Deleting Albums

Deleting an Album that you have created will simply remove the Album and its corresponding grouping of photos.

The photos in the album will still exist in the Photos library and in any other Album in which they have been placed.

If you want to delete an Album, just right-click on it in the Sidebar or on its thumbnail and choose '**Delete Album**'

Organising your Photos - Managing Albums

Sorting Photos within an Album

Photos within an album that you create can be sorted manually, or can be sorted automatically by title, or date-taken.

Just right-click on the album name and choose **Sort**. Then choose the desired sort option as shown in the below image.

If you would like to manually sort your photos, just ensure that no options are ticked in the Sort option. To 'untick', just click on the option that is ticked.

If none of these 'automatic sort' options are ticked, you will be able to drag photos into the order you require. In this case, photos added to the album will appear at the end of the album's photos, ready to be re-arranged.

Note that the Sort options are also available from the **View** menu.

Grouping Albums into Folders

Over time, you may find that you end up with a very long list of Albums – and need to be able to group these Albums together, and perhaps 'hide' the albums you are not currently using.

In the Photos app, it is possible to set up a whole structure of folders and sub-folders for storing Albums.

Folders don't store photos, so you can't drag photos into a folder. A folder can only contain albums and other folders.

To create a Folder, simple choose **File -> New Folder**.

Organising your Photos - Managing Albums

The new folder will appear under **My Albums**, with the name **Untitled Folder**. As for albums, this name can then be changed

If you had clicked on an existing folder in your **My Albums** list before choosing the **New Folder** option, then the new folder will be created inside the folder that you had selected.

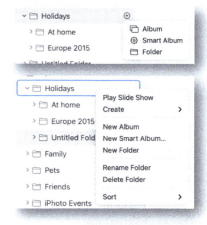

Alternative ways of creating folders

As we saw for Albums, there are a few other ways to create folders.

Choose the + symbol that appears when you click on **My Albums** or any of your already-created folders.

Or right-click on **My Albums** or any existing folder and choose **New Folder**

Populate your folder

Once the folder is created, drag albums or other folders on top of this new folder to move them to that folder.

Any folder containing albums or other folders will show $>$ on the left.

Click this symbol to expand the folder and see its contents.

Click the downward arrow $\vee$ to 'collapse up' the contents of the folder.

Creating a Folder Structure

To create folders within folders, simply drag one folder on top of the other.

You can create a multi-level folder structure, helping to keep all those albums easy to find.

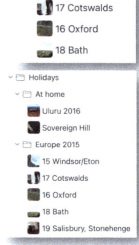

Organising your Photos - Managing Albums

When using the Sidebar, you can also right-click on any Folder and choose New Folder to create a folder within that folder.

In the example on the at the bottom of the previous page, I can easily find the holiday photos that I took in Italy when we travelled to Europe in 2015.

Renaming Folders

Renaming and re-arranging folders can be done in the same way as described above for Albums.

To rename, just right-click on the folder name and choose **Rename Folder**.

Alternatively, select the folder then click again on the name to get into 'edit' mode to change the name.

Deleting Folders

Right-clicking on the folder name also gives the **Delete Folder** option.

Deleting a folder will simply remove the folder and any folders and albums it contains.

The photos that were in the folders albums will still exist in the photo library.

Rearranging and sorting Folders

Drag folders around to manually re-order.

To automatically sort folders (or folders/albums within folders), right-click on the folder name or on the **My Albums** heading to choose the **Sort** option.

Choose to sort by **By Name**, **By Oldest First** or **By Newest First**.

Sharing Photos and Videos

The Photos app allows the sharing of the photos (and videos) from your Photos Library, using email, Messages, iCloud, Facebook and Airdrop. You can also add them to Notes, set an image as your Desktop picture, and more.

You can choose to share an individual photo or video, or several at once (although limits apply in certain cases).

Sharing photos or videos

Choose one or more photos (or videos) using the method described earlier in **Select Photos**

Then click 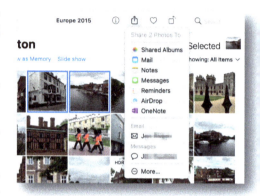 at top right to uncover your set of 'Share' options.

Click on the required 'Share' option from the list shown.

Depending on what Apps you have on your Mac, you may be able to add additional 'share' apps by clicking on the **More...** option.

Emailing photos

Choose the **Mail** option in share to send one or more photos via email.

If you send multiple images, just make sure that the email you are creating is not too big to send.

The size of the email is shown in **Message Size.**

If the email with images is over 500KB in size, you will be given the option to send the images as a smaller size.

Sharing Photos and Videos

The file size of the photos that you send can be adjusted using the **Image Size** field on the right side. Just click on this to see the various sizes that you can send, and to choose that which will apply to the current email. The **Message Size** will adjust when you change the **Image Size**.

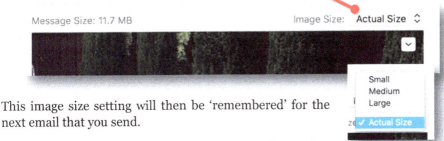

This image size setting will then be 'remembered' for the next email that you send.

This means that, if you adjust the size to Medium when sending a set of photos via email today, then the next time you create an email with photos, they will be automatically sized as Medium.

This can then be changed if you require a different sizing next time around – and will again be 'remembered'.

Sharing Photos with others via iCloud

A set of photos can also be shared using your iCloud, by setting up **Shared Albums.**

We will cover this in more detail later in this guide, as it gets us into the more complex territory that is iCloud!

Sharing photos using Airdrop

If you are looking to share photos or videos with another Apple user who is nearby (i.e. a matter of metres away), *Airdrop* allows for such sharing with other Apple devices (Mac, iPad and iPhone) without requiring internet access – using Bluetooth instead.

This can be very handy for a sharing a large group of photos or videos, avoiding size limits that may apply to email or messages and other sharing that requires internet access.

This is covered in more detail in part 2 of this guide series – **Files, Folders and Finder**.

Viewing your photos as a Slideshow

The **Slideshow** option allows your Photos app to automatically cycle through an album or set of photos, showing your images/videos.

You can have fancy 'transitions' and can even play your show with music – your own music, if you so desire.

The Slideshow option is available when you are viewing thumbnails of photos in an Album, and in certain other views. Look for the word Slideshow.

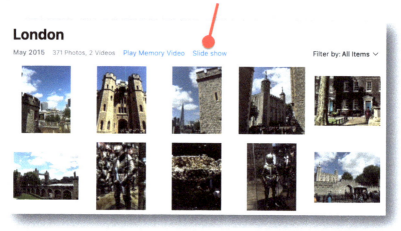

You will be given some options for presenting your slideshow – the 'theme' and the 'music'.

The **Theme** will determine the 'style' of the slideshow – try out each theme to work out which one suits.   A preview of the theme (and the default music that will play with it) will show in the small window above the theme names.

If you have any music in your iTunes library, you may be able to choose a single track to play with your Slideshow (instead of the default music).

Just choose the **Music** option at the top to see the music that you can choose from. Only

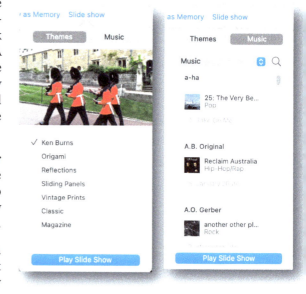

Viewing your photos as a Slideshow

music that is stored on your Mac can be chosen for your slideshow – Apple Music cannot be used.

When you have finished setting up your Slideshow, just click the **Play Slideshow** button to enjoy your slideshow!

You will also find the **Play Slideshow** option when you right-click (or two-finger-click) on an album or folder.

Creating a more customised slideshow

It is also possible to create a 'saved slideshow' Project, which allows for the re-ordering of photos, different transitions, text slides and captions and more.

The best way to create a Saved Slideshow is to first create an Album that contains the photos that you want to include in your Slideshow.

Then, just right-click (or two-finger-click) on the album in the sidebar or on the thumbnail of the album, and choose **Create**, then **Slide show**, then **Photos**.

This will create a slideshow Project in the **Projects** section and give this project the same name as the Album. It will include all the photos that are in the Album.

A slideshow project can also be created from a set of selected photos. Again, just right-click (or two-finger-click) on the selection to see the **Create** option, the **Slideshow**.

There are lots of additional options for then customising this Slideshow 'project'. Why not give it a go?!

Importing Photos into your Photos Library

There is a variety of ways to get photos into your Photos library. Some, like iCloud Photos (discussed later), happen automatically. Others involve imports from external devices, or files and apps on the Mac.

Import Photos from an iPhone or iPad

Using the cable that came with the Apple mobile device, connect the device to the USB port on your computer.

If the iDevice is not on, turn it on. Make sure you unlock it with your passcode.

If the iDevice pops up a message asking if the device should 'Trust' the computer, confirm the **Trust** option. You may also be asked to enter your device's passcode to confirm that the computer can be trusted.

The **Photos** app should open automatically. If it doesn't, click the **Photos** app in the Dock to open it. Your device will show under the **Devices** section of the sidebar.

The photos and videos on the device will be analysed, and you will be shown which are already in the Photos library (the **Already Imported** section), and those that are not yet in the Photos library (in the **New Photos** section).

- Import only some photos – click the photos you want to import, then choose the **Import Selected** button.

- Import all new photos from your camera - click the **Import All New Photos** button to do this.

Importing Photos into your Photos Library

Before you Import

There is another thing to decide before you click either of the above-mentioned **Import** buttons.

You can choose to import the photos to a specific album – either a new album or an existing album. Click the down-arrow of the **Import to** field to see the list of options.

If no choice is made here for an 'import to' album, the set of imported photos will still be able to be viewed in the **Imports** view that is found in the Photos section of the sidebar – and, if needed, selected and added to an album at some point after the import.

If the Photos app did not open automatically when you plugged in the mobile device, tick the '**Open Photos**' option at the top to ensure that the Photos app automatically opens next time the device is plugged in.

Another choice to make here is whether you want to keep the photos on the other device after they are imported. If you don't, tick the **Delete items** option on the right, under the Import options.

After the import process is finished, it is safe to disconnect the mobile device's USB cable without the need to 'eject' it.

Importing Photos into your Photos Library

Import photos from a digital camera

Using the cable that came with the camera, connect the camera to the USB port on your computer. (If your Mac has an SD card slot or you have a card reader, you can insert the SD card into that slot.)

For a connected camera, if the camera is not on, turn it on, and make sure it is set to the correct mode for importing photos. For information on which mode to choose, see the instructions provided with your camera.

If your camera has a "sleep" mode, make sure it is disabled or set to a time increment long enough to allow your images to download.

Open the Photos app, if it is not already open or it does not open automatically.

The import process is then the same as described for your Apple mobile device.

With SD cards and cameras connected to the Mac using a USB cable, make sure you safely eject before removing the card/cable. Click on the symbol ⏏ on the right of the device in Finder to do this.

Import photos from internal/external storage

If you have photos saved on your computer's hard drive (if, for example, you scanned photos or downloaded photos from an email), you can import them into Photos.

The same applies if the files are on a USB Flash drive (USB stick) or an external portable hard disk drive.

Importing can be achieved in a few ways

Method 1: With both the Finder and Photos visible, drag one or more photos or a folder of photos from the Finder onto the **Library** option in the Photos app's sidebar, or onto an album that you have created.

If duplicates are detected, you will be asked if you want to continue importing the photos or to 'skip' duplicates. Choose **Apply to all duplicates** if you wish your choice to apply to all the photos you are importing.

Importing Photos into your Photos Library

Method 2:   Drag one or more photos or a folder of photos from the Finder to on top of the **Photos icon in the dock**.

Method 3:   In Photos, choose **File->Import...**, then find and select the photos you want to import, then and click **Review for Import**.

Methods 2 and 3 two will give a similar 'Import' screen to that which applied for mobile device and camera imports. Method 1 does not give you any such screen – it simply imports the photos (as long as it doesn't need to ask about duplicates).

Once again, choose to import all new photos, or select a subset and **Import Selected**.

You may also notice a new checkbox, **Keep Folders,** below the 'Import' buttons.

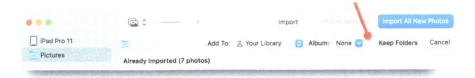

If this checkbox is ticked, the photos that you import will retain any folder structure that existed in Finder.

As an example, importing a Finder folder with 3 sub-folders (image on right) results in the creation of equivalent folder and sub-folders in the My Albums area of Photos, with the albums given the same name as the folder holding the photos (bottom image on right).

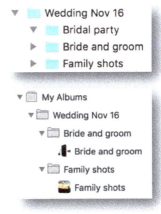

This is a great feature for anyone who has already organised their photos into folders on either Windows or a Mac, and who wants to keep that same organisation when the photos are imported to the Photos app, as folders and albums in Photos.

Importing Photos into your Photos Library

Import photos from a second Photos Library

macOS Monterey introduced the ability to import all photos from a separate Photos Library – something that was very difficult to do previously.

The way in which this is done is the same as just described above for importing photos from other locations on your Mac's hard drive or an external device.

The only difference is that, instead of selecting a folder or a selection of images to import, you instead select the applicable *.photoslibrary* file.

For example, if I use the Method 3 described in the previous sub-section, I can locate and select the other Photos library file (which could be either on my Mac's hard drive or on an attached external device) and then choose **Review for Import**.

It is important to note that this only imports the photos – and not any organisation (Albums) of those photos that you may have already done in that other Photos library.

Choose whether to store photos in the Photos Library when Importing

Before you import the photos from your Mac or external storage device, you can choose whether you want your photos actually stored in your Photos Library on your Mac. (Normally you would definitely choose to copy to the Photos library.)

This is done in the Photos Settings.

➢ Go to **Photos->Settings->General** (first option along top)

➢ Tick or untick the '**Copy items to the iPhoto Library**'.

Importing Photos into your Photos Library

If you choose not to copy the photos to the Photos Library, they will be left in their original location and the Photo Library 'database' will know to look for them there (instead of in the photos library database where they would normally 'live').

In this case, the 'source' of the photos must be available when you use the Photos app. If that source is an external storage device, the device must be plugged in and available.

One key limitation of choosing to <u>not</u> copy the photos into the Photos library relates to iCloud Photos. Photos that are stored outside the Photos library **cannot be sync'd to iCloud Photos**.

If you choose to **Copy items to the Photos Library**, you may then be able to delete the copied photos from the original location (unless you really want to keep them as a backup in that other location).

Save Photos directly from email, Message, or web page

A photo received in a mail message can be directly exported to Photos. 'Right- click' on the photo (or select more than one by holding the Command key as you click the photos) and choose the **Export to Photos** option.

The same applies for photos in your Messages – except the option is **Add to Photos Library**.

Similarly for web pages, photos you find in Safari may also be able to be saved to your Photos library.

Right-click (or two-finger-click) on a web page's photo, and (if it is available) choose the **Add Image to Photos** option.

You will then be able to find any photo that you add in this manner as the last in the **Photos** album.

It will appear in the **Year, Months** and **Days** timelines according to the date and time information recorded against each photo, and as the last photo (until another is added to Photos) in **Recent**.

Where do my photos 'live'?

The photos you see in your Photos App are held in a special file that usually lives in your **Pictures** folder on your Mac. Open **Finder** to see this folder

If you don't see the **Pictures** folder in your **Finder** sidebar, visit **Finder's Settings.**

Click the **Sidebar** option along the top and ensure the **Pictures** item is ticked.

(While you are there, turn on any other folders that you want to see as your Favourites in the Finder sidebar.)

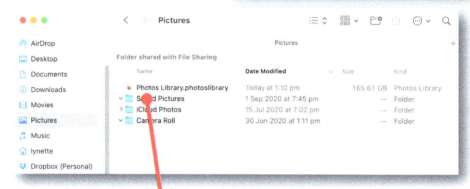

In the Pictures folder is a special file called **Photos Library.photoslibrary** (or you may see it as **Photos Library),** which contains your Photos Library and its database.

Whenever you open the Photos app in the Dock, it will look for this special file and show you its contents.

Double-clicking on the **Photos Library** file in the Pictures folder of Finder will also open that library using your Photos App.

Where do my photos 'live'?

Storing your Photos Library elsewhere

In saying that Pictures is the usual location of the Photos Library, this library does not have to 'live' in this particular location.

In fact, your Photos Library could be stored anywhere on your Mac, or even on an External Hard Disk Drive.

This can be especially handy if you don't have much storage capacity on your Mac and want to keep your photos stored elsewhere.

If you do store your Photos Library on an external device, that device must be plugged in whenever you open the Photos app.

More than one Photos Library

You can even have more than one **Photos Library**, and can open any alternative Photos Library by simply double-clicking on the applicable **Photos Library** file in Finder

Your Photos app will 'remember' which library was last opened and will open the same one again if the Photos app is selected from the Dock.

If you do have more than one Photo Library, only one library can be the 'main' library used as your 'system' library and by your iCloud.

In **Photos -> Settings**, the **General** option (top left) shows the location of the **Photos Library** you are currently using.

If the current library is not the 'system' photo library, you do have the option to make this alternative library into the main library by choosing **Use as System Photo Library** (which will be available if you are currently viewing an alternate photo library).

In the example on the right, the option is greyed because I am currently using the System Photo Library.

Be very careful about changing this though! If you have been sync'ing with iCloud, you will be messing around with this - something you may not wish to do!

Editing Photos

What sort of Editing is possible?

Quite often, the photos that we take can be made so much better with some minor (or major!) adjustments.

The following editing capabilities are provided by the Photos app on your Mac:

- Adjust the colour, light, and various other aspects of the photo including retouching and removing red eyes.
- Apply a range of filters to enhance your photo and change its 'look'
- Crop and adjust alignment
- Rotate
- Auto enhance
- Other edits using 'Extensions' from other apps.

We will look at each of these editing features in turn shortly.

Before we talk about the editing options, it is important to note that the edited photo does not replace the original photo. Your edited photo can be reverted to its original state at any time.

How do I get to the editing options?

When you are viewing an individual photo, you will see the **Edit** option at the top right of the screen.

Editing Photos

Just select any of the editing options to make the necessary changes to your Photo and choose **Done** at top right when you have completed editing.

Once you have applied any of these editing options, you will notice the **Revert to Original** option appears at top left, to allow you to go back to your un-edited version of the photo at any time.

Along the top of the Edit screen is a toolbar. We'll first look at the **Adjust**, **Filters** and **Crop** options.

Adjust

Clicking on the **Adjust** option gives a long list of options on the right-hand side of the screen, as shown in the image on the right.

These options allow you to adjust lighting, colour, remove flaws, correct 'red-eye' and more.

Editing Photos

On the left-hand side of each edit option is a > that can be clicked to expand that edit option.

For **Light, Colour** and **Black & White** options, you will see a 'slider' that allows for the manual adjustment of this aspect of the image.

Simply drag the vertical bar to adjust the lighting level, colour level or black & white level up and down.

For more 'granular' adjustments, choose the 'down-arrow' next to the word **Options**, which appears for each of these first three options.

Once you have adjusted any of these settings, a tick will appear on the right of the applicable adjustment.

To disable an adjustment, just remove this tick.

Re-apply the adjustment by ticking again – and your previous adjustments will be remembered.

To reset any of the adjustments, click the 'back-arrow' that appears on the left of the tick.

I'll leave those of you who are more advanced photo editors to have a play with these options and work out what they all do!

For those of you looking for easy adjustments to your photo, choose the **Auto** setting for each adjustment type and see the effect it has.

You can always use Command-Z to undo the applied adjustment.

Editing Photos

Retouch

I love this one! Retouch allows you to remove unwanted objects or defects from your photo. It can even help smooth out those wrinkles! Have a play with this option to get the hang of it!

Here is an example of a photo that I have quickly and easily 'retouched' to remove the dog and the school badge.

Expand the **Retouch** option by clicking the ▸.

You will see a **Size** slider, which allows you to set the size of the 'dot' ◯ that you will use to retouch your photos.

In the example on the previous page, I set the slider to about midway (to give a medium sized circle), then first 'Option-clicked' on the couch area above the dog.

This set the replacement 'dot' that would be used when I clicked and dragged over the dog. I had to click and drag a few times to get the required effect.

I then did the same thing with the jumper, option-clicking on a blue patch of jumper then clicking several times on the jumper logo to remove it.

Editing Photos

In the below photo, you see the instructions that appear, then disappear for the 'retouch' option.

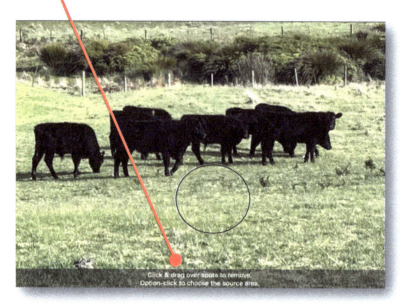

Click & drag over spots to remove.
Option-click to choose the source area.

Red Eye

We've all seen those photos taken with a flash, where the person in the shot looks like they are possessed – with red eye/s.

Your Mac allows you to remove red eyes from photos really easily.

Just click on ＞ on left of **Red Eye** and you will see some additional options, as shown on the right.

My favourite is the **Auto** option, which will automatically detect and remove any red eye issues in the photo.

If you are not happy with the Auto results, adjust the slider to approximate the size of the red eye, and click on each of the problem eyes to see if you get a better result.

Hopefully your subject won't end up looking too demonic!

Editing Photos

Other adjustments

The Photos app includes a wide range of other adjustments – white balance, levels, curves, selective colour, definition, noise reduction, sharpen and vignette. I won't go through what each of these means and does – but those of you who are avid photographers will hopefully be familiar with these options and what they do.

Editing Photos

Filters

Filters provides a way of changing the colours and tones of your image with a number of special effects, such as black and white, faded, a 'polaroid' look, and a few others.

Click on **Filters** (at top) to see the different options available on the right.

To choose a different effect for your photo, just click on one of the filters.

If you like that 'look' and wish the save the photo with this new effect, click **Done** at the top right.

To put your photo back to its original, unfiltered look, choose the **Original** filter at the top of the list.

Crop

The **Crop** feature of Edit mode allows you the change the borders of the photo – to cut out part of the photo or zoom in on the main area of interest.

It also allows for the straightening of your photo, or 'flipping'.

Click on **Crop** and you will see a border appear with 'tabs' at each corner.

You will also notice a 'wheel' on the right of the image that can be used to adjust the angle of the photo.

Just drag wheel up and down to 'turn' this wheel and adjust the angle of the photo.

Editing Photos

To crop the photo, simply drag the corners. You can then move the photo around within the adjusted 'frame' to adjust the positioning of the photo's features.

Something to thing to consider before you crop is whether you want to maintain the same '**Aspect ratio**' for the image – which means keeping or changing the shape and proportions.

To adjust this, just click **Aspect** to see the set of options shown on the right.

Choose the required Aspect. **Original** will set the proportions based on the original size (i.e. if it was a standard 4x6 photo, the shape will be adjusted accordingly).

Drag the photo around within the new framed area to adjust the positioning of the features of the photo within the frame.

At any point, the changes can be undone using the **Reset** option at the bottom.

Use the **Auto** button at the bottom to automatically straighten a crooked image.

You will also see that there are the **Straighten**, **Vertical** and **Horizontal** options at the top. Use these if you need to adjust the perspective of an image.

To complete any cropping and/or straightening you have applied, choose **Done** at top right.

Editing Photos

More options

There are a few other options available in Edit mode, and these are found on the top right-hand side of the edit screen, to the left of the **Done** options.

Quick Enhance

The **Quick Enhance** magic wand can provide a quick-fix for a not-so-great photo.

It balances the darks and lights and improves the contrast and brightness.

Just click on the magic wand symbol on the left of the **Done** option to see what a difference it makes.

Click it again to 'undo' this quick enhancement

Rotate

You will sometimes find that your photo has the wrong 'orientation', so is not able to be viewed in full screen mode or requires you to stand on your head to view it!

Click on the **Rotate** option to rotate the image 90° anti-clockwise. Keep clicking **Rotate** until your image is oriented correctly.

Extensions

For most Mac users, clicking on the extensions option will only give options **Markup** and **More...**

If you have any photo editing apps on your Mac, the **More** option will allow you to access any 'extensions' (i.e. a set of tools) that those apps provide for the Photos app.

Markup is a very handy option (added in MacOS Sierra) that allows you to 'draw on' an image, add a text box, and perform various other 'markup' operations.

Choose **Save Changes** when you are done.

Editing Photos

Compare your 'before' and 'after'

Once you have edited your photo in any way, you will see another option that appears just to the right of the traffic lights.

Click and hold on see the image before you applied the changes.

Let go to see the 'after' again.

If you are not happy with what you have done, choose **Revert to Original** on the right of that symbol.

Copy and Paste Edits (new in macOS Ventura)

A new editing feature available in macOS Ventura is the ability to copy the edits you have made to a particular photo and paste them across a range of other photos.

Apply the edits to your first photo and choose Done to complete these edits. Then, right click on the photo and choose **Copy Edits** (or choose the same option from **Image** menu at top).

Then, select the photo (or photos) to which you want to apply the same Edit. Right click on selected photo and choose **Paste Edits** (or choose the same option from the **Image** menu at top).

Note that this 'Copy and Paste Edits' feature does not work for Cropping of images.

Viewing/changing information about your Photo

It can be very useful to view the information about your photos, to find out things like

- The size of your photo
- When it was taken
- What device took it
- Location
- Identified people in photos

It is even possible to adjust date, time and location data stored against a photo. All of this information is known as the 'metadata' of the photo.

Let's look at the ways you can view and edit this 'metadata'.

The Info option

While viewing an individual photo, you will see the ⓘ option in the set of options at the top right.

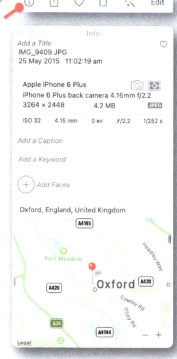

Click this symbol, or right-click on any photo and choose **Get Info**.

The metadata associated with the photo or video is shown in a separate window, including a map with the photo location (if this information is stored against the photo's).

If any 'faces' are found in the photo, you will have the chance to allocate a name to each face (for any that don't yet have a name).

Also available are some fields that can be added and edited by you - Title, Description, Keywords, faces.

Including these pieces of additional information about your photos and videos provides further ways of viewing, searching and organizing your photos and videos.

Viewing and changing information about your Photo

Identify Faces in a photo

Choosing the + option in the Faces section of the info screen will add a new 'circle' to your photo, one that can be placed over the face of an unidentified person, and then allocated a name. (We covered the People album earlier in this guide.)

Add or change a photo's location

Location information can be added later to any photo or video - very useful if you forgot to turn on Location Services on your iPhone or iPad, or if your camera does not have GPS capability.

In the Info view, click **Assign a Location** and then start typing the location – city, street address, country, or attraction. You will see suggestions from Maps appear – select the one that applies to your photo or video.

This will then allow your photo (or video) to be shown on a map, in the Places album, and in other areas of your Photos app that show maps.

Changing a Photo's date and time

In some situations, it is desirable to modify the date/time information stored about a photo (or a video).

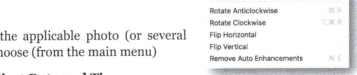

To do this, select the applicable photo (or several photos) and then choose (from the main menu)

Image -> Adjust Date and Time

This will show a screen that allows the adjusted time to be set, as well as the time zone applicable to the photo.

Viewing and changing information about your Photo

It is important to note that the original details of the photo are not lost when this is done and can be restored at any point if required.

This edit option is great for old hard-copy photos that you scanned into digital format, and that have the 'date scanned' as their adjusted date.

Setting an adjusted date that is closer to the date the photo was taken will allow them to appear in the correct year/month/day of your timeline.

Visual Lookup

You may notice that the ⓘ has a little star on it, as shown in the image on the right. In this case, there is also a little 'paw' symbol in the middle of the screen.

These symbols show that there is a subject in the photo for which you can lookup further information.

For the example on the right, when I click the 'paw', I get the screen on the right – providing information about the breed of dog.

This works for plants, flowers, art, landmarks and more. Give it a try if you see it!

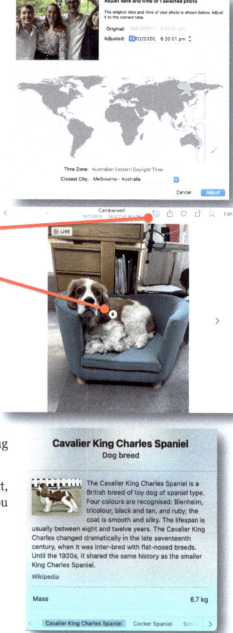

72

Trimming & Editing Videos

The videos that you stored in your Photos library can be very easily trimmed, to remove unneeded footage from the start or end.

Choose **Edit** to make apply any necessary Edits. You will see a bar along the bottom.

Just drag the left edge of the bar to the right and/or the right edge of the bar to the left to trim the start and end.

Once you are finished, choose **Done** (top right) to complete the trimming process. Easy!

If you decide that you want your untrimmed video back, just choose Edit again and the **Revert to Original** option (which will be available if there has been a trim performed previously).

With Big Sur and Monterey, there are some new video editing options available from the **Edit** option.

Adjust lighting, colour, white balance and more – similar options to that which apply to photos.

When you are finished with the video edits, choose **Done** and then choose whether you want to Save (and replace) the video, or whether you want it saved as a 'new clip'.

Remember that even if you choose Save Video, you can always revert to the original later if needed.

Duplicating photos and videos

On occasion, it may be necessary the take a copy of a photo – perhaps before you apply some edits, so that you can keep both the edited and unedited versions of the photo side by side.

First select one or more photos using the method described earlier in the guide.

When one or more photo/s is selected, you will find the **Duplicate** option as follows:

- Choose **File->Duplicate n Photo(s)**

- Right-click (or two-finger-click on the selected photo/s) and choose **Duplicate n Photo(s)**

The duplicated photo/s will keep the same date/s, time and location information as the original/s.

Albums and Folders can be duplicated too

If you ever need to duplicate an album or folder that you have created, just right-click (two-finger-click) on it and choose the **Duplicate** option that appears in the list.

Use Duplicates to keep modified AND unmodified versions

Duplicating a photo – either before or after you have edited it – allows you to retain the 'unedited' as well as the 'edited' versions of the same photo.

If the edits have already been applied, duplicate the photo then choose **Edit** for one of the versions of the photo, and choose to **Revert to Original**.

The two versions of the same photo will then sit alongside each other in the 'timeline' view represented by the Library option.

Searching for photos

When you are viewing thumbnails of photos (i.e. you are not viewing an individual photo), there will always be a **Search** field showing at the top right.

This **Search** feature allows for searching for photos/videos based on a wide range of search criteria.

- Place
- Person/Face
- Date or Date range
- Keyword, Title, Description (if you have any of this user-specified data recorded against your photos)
- Category - e.g. Christmas Tree, Tree, Water, Dog, Cat, etc.

Below, you can see what I get if I type the letters 'dog' into my search field – a set of photos with dogs, Moments that include dogs, Albums referring to dogs, a variety of categories for dog, and places. Choose **See All** at the top right of some of the sections on this screen to view all photos represented by the section.

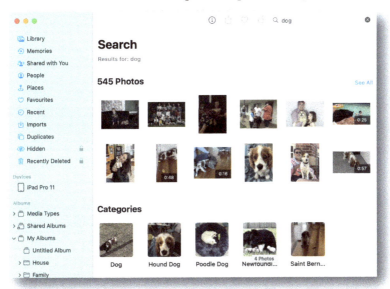

Having found a set of photos that match your search criteria, you can then quickly create an album containing the photos that match.

Such an album can then be used as part of the rules for a Smart Album (see next section).

Organising your Photos - Smart Albums

We have previously covered how to create your own Albums of photos – and how to go about adding photos to those albums.

These standard albums only contain the photos that you choose to put into the album.

There is another type of album that can be created, one that can determine its contents automatically based on a set of 'rules' that you define.

These are called **Smart Albums**.

Creating a Smart Album

As an example, you could set up a Smart Album that includes all videos that were taken in a date range.

To create a Smart Album, choose
File -> New Smart Album.

You will see the following screen, where the rule or rules for your Smart Album can be defined.

Give your Smart Album a name in the first field, then choose the first condition.

Click on each of the selection boxes to choose the basis of your rule – on the left is the list of attributes that can be used for the rule.

In my case, I will set up my first condition to look for 'photos' that have type 'movie', and the second condition to look for items with a 'date' in the past 30 days.

Organising your Photos - Smart Albums

I chose the + symbol on right of the first conditions to create a second condition. If I need to remove a condition, I use the -.

I have also set my rule to require that 'all' of the conditions are true for a photo to be included (instead of 'any').

Once I choose OK, a new Smart Album will appear in my Albums area, with the chosen name.

Viewing Smart Albums

Smart Albums are listed in your set of Albums, and are indicated by the symbol on the left side

The contents of the Smart Album are determined by the rule, so it is not possible to 'drag' or manually add photos to the Smart Album.

The Smart Album's contents will change dynamically based on the photos that are currently in your library – those that meet the Smart Album's rule/s will be automatically added.

If a photo that was previously in the Smart Album is deleted, it will be automatically deleted from the Smart Album.

Sorting, editing, duplicating, and deleting a Smart Album

Various options relating to the Smart Album are available by right-clicking (two-finger-clicking) on the album.

Choose **Edit Smart Album** to change the album's rules.

The name can also be changed in the same way, by choosing the **Rename Smart Album** option.

Sort the contents of the Smart Album using the Sort option. And, of course, you can **Duplicate** and **Delete** the Smart Album.

Exporting Photos

On occasion, you may find it is necessary to export a set of photos from your Photos app – say to a USB stick or external hard drive.

Exporting of a selection of photos can be achieved as follows:

- Select your photos

- Choose **File –> Export**

- You will see there is the option to
  Export xx Items ... or
  Export unmodified Original for xx items...

- The first option will export the 'modified' version of your photo/s, including any edits, face allocations, adjustments to date/time and location, and any title/description/keyword additions.

- Each photo will retain the 'date and time taken' metadata associated with each photo/video, **BUT** the 'date created' and 'date modified' that shows in Finder for each image file will be the date and time that the export occurred. This can be very frustrating if you want to see the real 'date taken' information in Finder.

- If you want to keep the date/time that the photo/video was taken in Finder, you will need to choose the second option - '**Export unmodified Original for xx items...**'. The disadvantage of this option is that any edits you have applied to your photo will not be included in the exported photo/s and video/s.

For the **Export xx Items ...** option you will see the screen on the right.

If you want to include Location information with the exported photos, tick the 'Location Information' option.

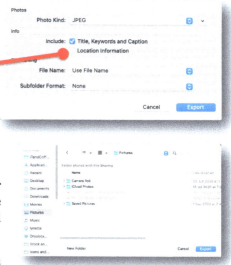

Choose **Export** when you are ready to choose the disk location for the exported items.

You will then see the standard Finder 'Save' screen, that allows you to choose where to save your exported photos/videos.

You can even create a **New Folder** in which to store the items.

78

Exporting Photos

Once you have chosen the location, click the **Export** button.

A slightly different, simpler export screen (right) appears if you chose the second option, **Export unmodified Original for xx items...**

Select **Export**, to again get the Finder 'Save' screen and complete the export process of the original versions of the photos.

Handy tip for exporting a selection of photos

If you have a random selection to export, it is best to set up an Album first.

Once your album is complete, click on a single photo or video 'thumbnail', then press **Command-A** to select all photos in the Album

Then choose **File -> Export**, and follow the steps described above.

Remember, if you Export the 'unmodified' photos, your photos keep date information when viewed in Finder.

Sorting out all those Duplicates

It is certainly not unusual to find yourself with lots of duplicate photos in your Photos Library.

Up until macOS Ventura, there was no built-in feature for discovering and sorting out duplicates.

macOS Ventura helps you find Duplicates

Apple has finally provided a feature that can detect and help you resolve the duplicated photos in your library. This new Ventura feature can locate exact copies (which could have different metadata), as well as photos that appear the same or similar.

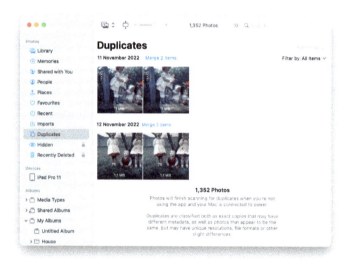

You can review the duplicates one-by-one and choose **Merge n Items** to resolve the duplication. The message shown on right will appear.

Or you can choose to Select All (Command-A) and choose the **Merge nnn Items** that appears at the top right of the screen – to resolve them or all in 'one fell swoop'.

Any photos deemed to be duplicates will be moved to the Recently Deleted album.

The great thing about this new feature is that any removal of duplicates will not impact your Albums – even if the photo in the album is the one being deleted. It will be replaced with the photo that is retained.

Where do my photos 'live'?

Third-party solutions

Another option is to purchase a 3rd-party product that allows you to sort out all those duplicates a lot more quickly.

Several years ago, I purchased a product called **PhotoSweeper,** available in the Mac App Store. This has served me very well in my quest to rid my library of the duplicates that creep in there on a regular basis.

Of course, there are many other products that do the same thing – for example

- Duplicate Photos Fixer Pro
- Duplicate File Finder Remover
- Cisdem Duplicate Finder +

This guide is not seeking to recommend any one of these products.

Your best bet is to Google reviews of products that manage duplicated photos on a Mac – and make your own assessment and purchase.

Photo Books

Up until 2018, there was the option to create a **Photo Book** within the **Photos App**. These photo books were printed by Apple.

At the end of September 2018, Apple ceased its Photo Book service.

The option to create a photo book is still available within the Photos app, but you will now have to install and use a third-party a photo book app from the **App Store**.

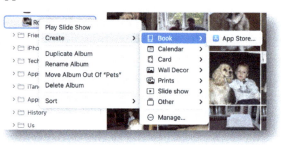

Selecting the option to create a book will redirect you to the App Store to choose an app.

As at the time of writing this guide, the only two apps available in Australia are **Mimeo Photos** and **MILK Handcrafted Photo Books**

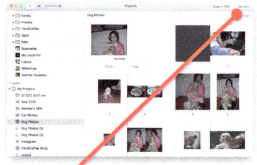

We won't go into detail in this guide about how to use any third-party product.

However, it is good to know that, if you have already started or completed a Photo Book using Apple's defunct service, it is possible to choose the **Convert** option at top right (when viewing your already-created photo book) and then choose the 3rd-party app you wish to use instead.

Alternatively, there are many other non-Apple services for creating photo books – Snapfish, Blurb, Shutterfly, Albumworks and Momento, just to name a few.

To create a card or calendar, or order prints:

The same Applies for other printed products that you used to be able to order from Apple. These must now be created and ordered through a third-party provider.

Now let's talk about Photos in iCloud

There are three aspects of iCloud that relate to your photos and videos. These are

- iCloud Photos
- My Photo Stream (not available for newer iCloud accounts)
- Shared Albums

For any of these options to be available in the Photos app, your Mac must be using iCloud.

To check if you are signed in to iCloud, go to your **System Settings**.

 -> **System Settings** -> **Apple ID** (first option at top of the left sidebar, showing your name if you are signed in).

Managing the various aspects of photos in iCloud can be done from the **Photos** app.

Go to **Photos -> Settings** and choose the **iCloud** option (at the top) to see the set of options in relation to iCloud.

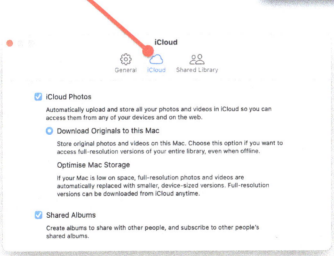

Next are the options for selecting the parts of iCloud that you wish to 'turn on' and show in your Photos app on the Mac.

We will then cover each of these areas in further detail in the next few sections of the guide.

Now let's talk about Photos in iCloud

iCloud Photos

Stores all your photos in iCloud and allows each of your devices to view and manage this same set of photos and Albums.

Extra iCloud storage may be needed to store large libraries, and devices that can't fit the entire library will need internet access when viewing any photos. (Note. Windows computers can also use iCloud Photos.)

iCloud Shared Photo Library

New in macOS Ventura are Shared Libraries, allowing you to share a whole library of photos with up to 5 people. We have an extended description of this feature coming up shortly.

Shared Albums

Allows creation of albums in iCloud, that can be then shared with other people.

These Shared Albums are separate to your iCloud Photos – so deleting a photo from your library will not delete it from any Shared Album (and vice-versa) you have added it to.

The great news is that Shared Albums do not add to your iCloud storage usage. A Shared Album can have up to 5000 items in it.

iCloud Photos

iCloud Photos was introduced in 2015. It provides cloud storage of all your photos in iCloud and allows the viewing and updating of the 'library' in iCloud from any devices connected to that iCloud account.

The great benefit of iCloud Photos

Photos and albums are synchronized between all Apple devices that are connected to the iCloud Photos – meaning that albums can be created on an iPhone, iPad and Mac, and be visible then on all other devices.

It also means that photos deleted on one device are also deleted on other devices. People albums sync, as do Favourites.

For many people (and I am one of them!), this offers a great solution to storage of their photos.

An even better reason to use iCloud Photos with macOS Ventura

As touched on earlier, macOS Ventura has brought us Shared Photo Libraries.

You can now set up an alternative library that you share with up to 5 other family members or close friends. You can choose for all your photos to go to this shared library – so that the other person/people can see them all – or if only the photos you choose should go to that library.

This now offers a great way of collecting together all the family photos in one place, accessible by all who want to see them.

We'll cover this new feature in more detail shortly.

The disadvantages of iCloud Photos

The problems start when your Photos library is a large one.

iCloud Photos offers only an 'all or nothing' solution to storage of your photos on each device. This means that, if iCloud Photos is turned on, the device will show EVERY photo and video that is in the library.

If your library is big, it may not fit on your mobile devices. It may not fit on your Macbook if it has only 128GB or 256GB of storage.

In this case, your device will store 'cut down' versions of your photos – versions that are 'blurry' and can only be viewed properly once they are downloaded from your iCloud.

iCloud Photos

In this case, you need internet access to view your photos, and have to endure a delay before you can see full resolution versions of your photos and videos.

This can result in unexpected mobile data usage, and great frustration at the delay in seeing a clear image, or at not being able to view photos when there is no internet.

If your iCloud Photos library does not fit on a device, the photo storage must be 'optimised'.

This is one of the options a that can be selected in **Photos -> Settings**, in the **iCloud** option.

Added to all this is the cost of storing all your photos in iCloud. If your Photos library is large, you will be looking at a higher iCloud subscription cost of $4.49 per month for 200GB or perhaps $14.99 per month for 2TB. (Australian $ shown here.)

Should you use iCloud Photos?

At the time of writing this guide, iTandCoffee's recommendation is that you don't set up iCloud Photos without considering the implications – especially if your devices don't have a lot of available storage capacity.

While I highly recommend it, I have assisted many people who have turned it on without understanding these implications and then had issues when trying to 'undo' this.

If iCloud Photos has been accidentally enabled, it can be tricky to undo – especially where you don't use iCloud Photo Library on your computer and want to import (using a USB cable) the photos from your iPhone or iPad.

You may find that the import process shows there are no photos to be imported, even though you know there should be.

The problem is that iCloud has the photos, but your mobile device only has the 'optimised' version of the photos (which can't be imported to the computer).

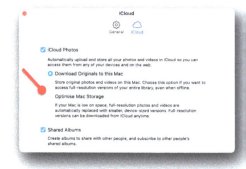

Refer later in this guide for details of what to do if your photos are in iCloud and you need to get them out of iCloud and onto your Mac.

iCloud Shared Photo Library

Share a Photos Library with family and/or friends

As mentioned above, macOS Ventura now allows the set up a central Shared iCloud Photos Library that can be seen and used by up to 5 other family members and/or friends.

You can only participate in one Shared library. Typically, this will be a Family shared library that all members of the family can use. And the person who creates the Shared Library must have sufficient iCloud storage for all participants. The photos in the Shared Library do not count towards participants' iCloud allowance.

For collections of photos that you share with different groups of people, Shared iCloud Albums are still available (see next section).

Create an iCloud Shared Photo Library

To get started, go to **Photos -> Settings**, to the **Shared Library** option along the top. Choose **Get Started ...**

You will then need to choose the family member/s or friend/s with whom you wish to share new library. Choose **Add Participant** to select one or more participants.

Very importantly here, you can only choose someone who is an Apple iCloud user, and who has chosen to use iCloud Photos. Choose **Continue** when after adding participants.

You will then be asked to choose how you wish to populate the new Shared Library. You can choose to share ALL your current photos and videos, choose certain people or a date range, or choose to manually select the photos to share (see screen on right).

I recommend choose the **Move Photos Later** option – so that you can be more selective

iCloud Shared Photo Library

about which photos to add to this shared library.

You will then be asked if you want to, at this point, share the invitation to join the Shared Library with those you have chosen (see leftmost image below). This can be done by sending them a Message (choose **Invite via Messages** button), or by choosing the **Copy Link** option at bottom left.

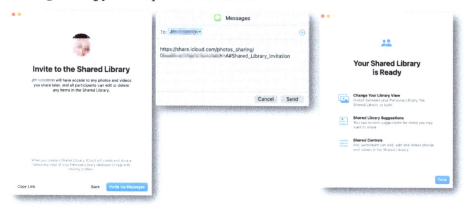

You will then get the screen shown above right – advising that your Shared Library is ready.

If you receive a Shared Library invitation ...

If you are the recipient of an invitation to share an iCloud Shared Photos Library, you will see the below left screen when you click the link.

Choose **Get Started**, then choose which photos you wish to add to that library. I suggest that, at this point, you choose the **Move Photos Later** option at bottom).

If you did select some photos to add to the library, you will get a Preview option (as shown in rightmost image above). Choose to preview, or choose Skip if you don't need to do this.

iCloud Shared Photo Library

You will then see the final confirmation screen, allowing you to confirm that you wish to **Join Shared Library**.

This confirmation shows the details of the Apple ID that you are joining as, and the number of photos you have chosen to move to the Shared Library initially.

You may also see the screen shown in the rightmost image above, asking if you want photos shared from your iPhone's (and iPad's) Camera.

I recommend choosing **Share Manually Only**, so that you have some control over what ends up in the Shared Library.

The final screen in the setup series confirms that your Shared Library is ready. Select **Done** to exit the setup process.

Manage Shared Library Settings

Future management of tha Shared Library can be done by the creator of the library by returning to **Photos -> Settings**, to the **Shared Library** option along the top (see image above right).

You can **Add Participants** (up to a total of 5), add photos of selected People, adjust some other settings and, if needed **Deleted Shared Library** (as long as you are the person who created the Shared Library).

If you do choose the Delete option, you will be asked what you want to do with the photos that are in the Shared Library – to **Keep Everything** or **Keep only what I contributed**.

iCloud Shared Photo Library

Choosing which Photos Library to View

Once a Shared Library has been created, you will notice a new control in the bar along the top – to the right of the Traffic Light – showing which library (or libraries) is currently visible. (It may just show a symbol, or include text – depending on the width of the window)

Click on this control to see the options available – to view the consolidation of both libraries, just your own Personal Library, or just the Shared Library.

If no participants have added any photos to the Shared Library, you will see the screen on the right, advising how to populate the new library.

Return to the view showing either Both Libraries or your Personal Library.

Add Photos to the Shared Library

Make sure you are viewing either Both Libraries or Personal Library.

Select one or more photo thumbnails, then right-click and choose **Move n Photos to Shared Library**.

You can also right-click on a single photo that you are currently viewing to see the same option.

Confirm by choosing the **Move** option from the confirmation screen.

When you are viewing Both Libraries, you will notice that photos that are in the Shared Library will have a 'people' symbol at top right of its thumbnail.

iCloud Shared Photo Library

Move your photos back to Personal Library

To move any of your photos out of the Shared Library and back to your Personal Library, select the photo/s, then right-click and choose **Move n Photos to your Personal Library.**

Automatically add photos to Shared Library from iPhone

We will not spend many words on this for the sake of this book about the Mac, but it is important to know that you can set up your iPhone and iPad to automatically (or manually) populate the Shared iCloud Photo Library when a photo is taken.

The relevant options for your iPhone or iPad can be found in the device's Settings app.

Go to **Settings -> *your-name* -> iCloud -> Photos -> Shared Library ->
Sharing from Camera** OR to
Settings -> Camera –> Shared Library.

  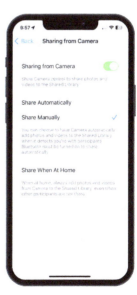

The screen above right shows the options available for sharing photos from the device's camera.

I choose to **Share Manually** and to turn off **Share When at Home**, as I only want certain photos to go into the Shared Library.

Shared Albums

Sharing Albums using iCloud

A set of photos can be shared with anyone, by using your iCloud and setting up **Shared Albums.**

Shared Albums allow you to share an album of photos with other iCloud users, AS WELL AS with other 'non-Apple' people – without using any additional iCloud storage allocation. Shared Albums can have up to 5000 photos or videos.

I use iCloud Shared Albums all the time to share photos of trips, family events and more.

Those who share the album with you can like, comment, or even add more photos to the Shared Album.

For this option to be available, you must ensure the following setup has occurred:

- Sign in to iCloud on your Mac - this is done in **System Settings -> Apple ID**

- Turn 'on' **Shared Albums** from **Photos -> Settings -> iCloud**

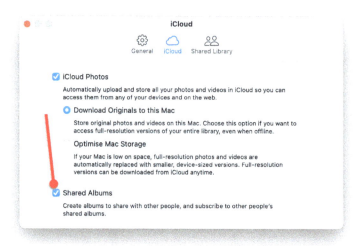

Having ensured that your Shared Albums option is active, it is then easy to share a set of photos via your iCloud.

- Select one or more photos (using the technique described earlier)
- Choose the Share symbol
- Or right-click on selected photos and hover mouse pointer over **Share**
- Choose the option **Shared Albums**

Shared Albums

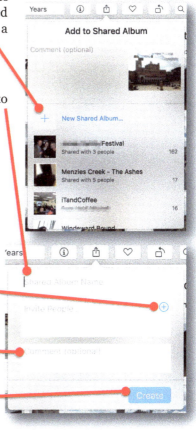

- Choose the existing Shared Album to which to add the photos – i.e. choose an existing Shared iCloud Album from the list shown or create a **New Shared Album**

- For a **New Shared Album**

  ○ In **Shared Album Name**, assign a name to the album,

  ○ In **Invite People**, enter the names of Contacts (they must be iCloud users who have also turned on the **Shared Album** option).

    As you start typing a contact name, it will appear in 'blue' if the contact is on iCloud.

    Alternatively, choose the blue + to see your Contacts list and choose the applicable (and iCloud-enabled) Contacts.

    You can skip inviting people at this point and do it later instead.

  ○ Add a **Comment** if you like

  ○ Select **Create** after you have selected all the required contacts that you would like to share with (if any).

Viewing Shared Albums

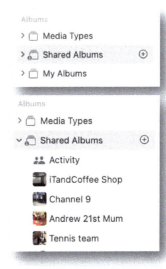

You can then view your Shared Albums in the **Shared Albums** area under the **Albums** section of Photos.

If you don't see anything listed in the Shared Albums click the > symbol on the left-hand side to expand.

The **Shared Albums** area of your Photos app shows those albums you shared with others and those that are shared with you.

The **Activity** option shows last added photos, comments and likes for all Shared Albums.

Shared Albums

Permanently saving photos from a Shared iCloud Album

Photos you see in the **Shared Albums** area are separate to those in the main Photos library.

Any photos not shared from your own Photos library (i.e. added by someone else) are not permanently stored on your device and will disappear if the Shared Album is deleted or you 'unsubscribe' (see later in this section).

If you wish to permanently save other peoples' photos that you have in the Shared Albums area, you need to **Import** them to your Photos library. (Only then can they be used in your Albums.)

Select the Shared photos you wish to import (using the selection method described earlier in this guide).

Right Click (or two-finger-click) on one of the selected photos and choose **Import**.

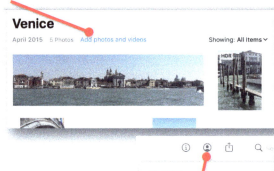

Adding photos or videos to a Shared Album

To add new photos to a Shared Album, select the Shared album then choose **Add photos and videos.**

Alternatively, use the same method described earlier – of selecting the photos first, then choosing the **Share** symbol and the **Shared Albums** option.

Click on an existing Shared Album to add the selected photos to that album.

Managing who can see your Shared Album

Add new subscribers to a Shared Album at any time by choosing the 'Person' symbol at top right. This symbol is visible when you select a Shared Album in the sidebar.

Change the name of the Shared album in the first field of the window that appears.

Shared Albums

The + symbol in the 'Invite People' frame allows additional people to be invited to subscribe to the album.

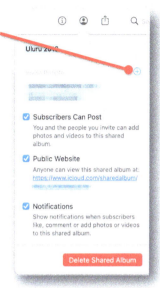

If there is someone you want to remove as a subscriber, just click the 'down-arrow' on the right of their name and choose the option 'Remove Subscriber'

You will see several other options in this screen

- Choose whether subscribers can add photos to the shared albums (**Subscribers can Post**)

- Option to create a '**Public Website**' that can be shared. This generates a link to a web page that will show your Shared iCloud Album's photos, a link that can be shared with those who don't use Apple or iCloud. Your iCloud album can then be viewed in any web browser using the shared link

- Choose whether you want **Notifications** popping up on your Mac about any activity in relation to album

Unsubscribing from an album someone else shared with you

If you no longer wish to see a Shared Album that someone else shared with you, just right-click (or two-finger-click) on it in the sidebar and choose **Unsubscribe from Shared Album**.

This will remove the album from the **Shared Albums** area on all your devices.

Deleting a Shared Album

If you no longer want to keep a Shared Album that you created, right-click and choose **Delete Shared Album**.

Alternatively, choose ⓘ in the top bar and select the **Delete Shared Album** option at the bottom of the window (see image at top right).

The Shared Album will be removed from the Shared Albums area on all your devices. Deleted shared albums also then disappear from Shared Albums area of any subscribers

How to get your Photos out of iCloud

If you have turned on **iCloud Photos** on your iPhone (or iPad), but not on your Mac (or Windows computer), you may find yourself in the situation where your photos are no longer stored on your mobile device - that they have been 'sucked up' into **iCloud Photos** instead.

As described earlier, this occurs in cases where there is insufficient room to store the photos on your mobile device, resulting in an 'optimised' **Photos** library on the device. When you view your photos on that device, they must be downloaded from iCloud - requiring internet access, and often resulting in a delay before you can view your full resolution photo.

Another consequence of an optimised Photos library on the iDevice may be that, when you plug your iPhone (or iPad) into your computer, you may be told that there are no photos to import - even though you know that you just took some new photos!

The problem is that they have been uploaded to iCloud and removed from the device to save space, before you can import them.

This can leave your photos in a 'no-man's-land', where they are not on your iPhone/iPad, and are not on your computer.

In this case, most people I see with this problem would choose to turn off the iCloud Photo Library option on their mobile device - so that they have more control over which photos are actually stored on their device, and don't have to rely on internet access to be able to view their photos.

The problem then is how to get the photos, that are then only stored in iCloud Photo Library, out of iCloud and onto their computer.

Before we look at options ...

Apple provides the **icloud.com** website, where you are able to see the content of your iCloud - including the content of your iCloud Photos.

You would think that logging into **icloud.com** would solve your problem - i.e. that you would be able to export your photos from there.

Unfortunately, there is currently no option to 'download all' photos. You can only download up to 1000 photos at a time. If you have a large number of photos to download, this may not offer a workable solution.

How to get your Photos out of iCloud

Turn on iCloud Photos in Photos on your Mac

On the Mac, you could turn on **iCloud Photo Library** in the **Photos** app's Settings (or in **System Settings -> iCloud -> Photos**) to get your iCloud-based photos downloaded to your computer.

In many cases, however, this is not the best idea.

If you already have a big photos library on your Mac, that library will first be uploaded to iCloud, perhaps requiring additional iCloud storage and, in many cases, a lot of time to complete the upload.

If you are not wanting to continue using iCloud Photo Library, you may want to get your photos out of iCloud without having to involve your current Photos Library.

A solution that doesn't involve uploading existing Photos Library

If you don't want to involve your current Photos Library, the best option is to create a second Photos Library and use it to get your photos out of iCloud.

Once the photos are downloaded to this second library, you can use the Export option to extract the photos and then Import them to the 'real' Photos Library.

Set up a second Photos Library

Setting up a second Photos Library is quite straight-forward.

Make sure your Photos app is closed.

Then, as you click the **Photos** app in the Dock, hold down the **Option** key.

This will provide the **Choose Library** screen. At the bottom of this screen, choose the **Create New** button.

Name your temporary Photos Library in the **Save As** field at the top (or just leave it with the default name) and click **OK.**

How to get your Photos out of iCloud

How to get the photos downloaded to this second library

You will then need to temporarily make this new library the **System Photo Library**, so that it is the main library that can interact with iCloud.

To do this, go to **Photos -> Settings** (in the menu bar at top left).

Click the **Use as System Photo Library** button in the **General** section. When you do this, the button becomes greyed to indicate this is now the System Photo Library.

Then select the **iCloud** option in the same **Settings** screen (at top of that screen).

Select/tick the **iCloud Photos** option and also ensure that the **Download Originals to this Mac** option is ticked.

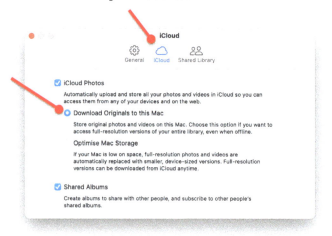

Then sit back and wait.

How long will the photos download take?

The time it then takes to download your photos to your Mac will depend on
- the number of photos in your iCloud Photos Library and
- the speed of your internet.

How to get your Photos out of iCloud

It may take days, so you will need to be patient - and leave your device connected to the internet so the download can complete.

How do I know if the download is complete?

If the message at the bottom, of the Photos or Moments view shows something like the message here, then your download is completed.

34,987 Photos, 1,383 Videos
Synced with iCloud Just Now

If the message instead shows that there are uploads or downloads in progress, then you will need to wait a bit longer.

When the download is completed, go back to your **Photos -> Settings** in the temporary Photos library and turn off (untick) **iCloud Photos**.

Merge the Photos Libraries

So, the download is complete - and you now have two Photos Libraries in the Pictures folder of Finder.

These libraries now need to be merged.

Open Original Photos Library again

Before you import the downloaded photos into the **original** photos library, you will need to re-instate it as the 'system photo library'.

To open the original Photos Library, hold the **Option** key again as you click the Photos app.

Choose the applicable file (which is usually called **Photos Library.photoslibrary**).

Go to **Photos -> Settings** and click the **Use as system photos library** button for this library.

(Note. If you don't intend to use iCloud Photos, also go to the **iCloud** option in Photos Settings and make sure that the **iCloud Photos** option is not ticked.)

Import downloaded photos to Original Photos Library

Then, go ahead with the **Import** of the folder/s of photos that you downloaded or the separate Photos library that you used for the download from iCloud – by choosing File -> Import, then choosing the alternative Photos Library file from the Pictures folder (as discussed earlier, on page 56)

Other Books in this Series

A Guided Tour

Files, Folders & Finder

Backups, Apps & Settings

All Sorts of Handy Tips

Videos about the Mac

Learn even more about your Mac with a range of Videos about the Mac, available on the iTandCoffee website.

For more information about iTandCoffee class videos and user guides, visit

www.itandcoffee.com.au/videos

www.itandcoffee.com.au/guides